A THEORY OF ECONOMIC–DEMOGRAPHIC

DEVELOPMENT

A THEORY OF
ECONOMIC–DEMOGRAPHIC
DEVELOPMENT

BY HARVEY LEIBENSTEIN

FOREWORD BY FRANK NOTESTEIN

GREENWOOD PRESS, PUBLISHERS
NEW YORK

FOREWORD

We hope that students of population will find this book a welcome innovation in the series of studies sponsored by the Office of Population Research. Partly from reasons of conviction, but mainly from a sense of research strategy, the four previous books dealing with populations of high fertility and mortality have been empirical studies. They are: Kingsley Davis, The Population of India and Pakistan (Princeton, 1951); T. E. Smith, Population Growth in Malaya (Chatham House, 1952); Paul K. Hatt, Backgrounds of Human Fertility in Puerto Rico (Princeton, 1952); and George W. Barclay, Population and Colonial Development in Taiwan (Princeton, 1954).

In contrast to the others, Professor Leibenstein has worked in pure theory. Using progressively enriched, but still highly simplified models, he examines some of the characteristics of the interplay of economic and demographic forces in situations in which both fertility and mortality are very high. The result is that he has made more rigorous the essentials of the Malthusian propositions, spelled out at least some of the conditions necessary for the destabilization of the Malthusian equilibrium, provided interesting suggestions for approaching the problems of choice without neglecting the normative order, and made suggestions concerning ways in which the optimum concept can be pointed in useful directions.

On the substantive side one of the more interesting propositions is what might be called "the critical minimum effort thesis" developed in Chapter IV. It is the idea that to achieve a destabilization of the underdevelopment equilibrium, the effort made, whatever its form, must be of a certain minimum magnitude in order to result in a lasting improvement in the level of living, and that otherwise whatever gains are made will be at best temporary.

My colleagues and I wish to express our gratitude to the

v

vi

Milbank Memorial Fund and The Rockefeller Foundation for the finan-
cial support that made this study and our other work possible, and
equally for the complete freedom given us in both the selection and the
execution of our research projects.

Frank W. Notestein
Director
Office of Population Research

PREFACE

The first version of this essay was written during the
year 1949-1950, and revised during the year following. Subsequent
revisions involved changes in form and mode of expression, but not
in content. After the first revision no attempt was made to keep track
of and to include in the text all the current literature that was appear-
ing on the subject. If the essay were written today portions of the
text would undoubtedly be different, but the approach to the problem
and the conclusions reached would be the same.

At one point during the process of revision the author
considered the possibility of relegating all mathematical arguments
and notation to appendices and footnotes. However, in view of the
fact that the algebra, where employed, is of an exceedingly elementary
nature, and that its elimination would have required a longer and much
more cumbersome verbal argument, the author thought it best to
leave the essay in its present form.

During the work on this study the author incurred a
number of intellectual debts not mentioned in the text. Although it
would be impossible to acknowledge all sources of help, inspiration,
and constructive criticism, some must be mentioned. This study
would never have been undertaken without the aid of the Office of
Population Research at Princeton University, through their provision
of a graduate fellowship, excellent working facilities, and extremely
congenial surroundings, and through the encouragement and guidance
of Frank W. Notestein, director of the Office. Various members of
the staff of the Office were very helpful, listening to portions of the
essay at Office seminars and offering valuable criticism, both solici-
ted and unsolicited. Professors Notestein, Friedrich Lutz, Oscar
Morgenstern, and Jacob Viner read the essay at various stages and
were exceedingly helpful in making suggestions and in pointing out

viii

shortcomings and difficulties. The anonymous readers of the Princeton University Press were helpful in a similar vein. Of course, none of those mentioned either explicitly or implicitly are responsible for any errors, omissions or lapses in logic that the manuscript may contain, and I add this not only because such disclaimers are conventional, but also because I was often singularly stubborn in accepting suggestions.

Harvey Leibenstein
Berkeley, California
June 15, 1953

TABLE OF CONTENTS

A THEORY OF ECONOMIC–DEMOGRAPHIC

DEVELOPMENT

CHAPTER I

INTRODUCTION

In the long run the course of economic development is inextricably bound up with changes in the size and composition of the population. In areas where unquestionable economic growth has taken place and where the level of living has increased these developments have usually been accompanied by unprecedented increases in population. In other areas where such expansion has not taken place and where levels of living have not risen it has been argued by some that this lack of development is due to population pressure; that is, that potential increases in average income, which can be brought about either by technical advances or by the introduction of new capital, are swallowed up by population increases. Whether or not such views are accepted depends on our notions about the factors that cause economic growth and foster improvements in the general level of living, and the relationship of these factors to population changes; or, in other words, on our understanding of the interaction between demographic and economic variables.

Today, the study of the interaction between such variables appears to be a neglected field compared to work done in other aspects of the social sciences. This is especially true with regard to the theoretical aspects of the problem. The reason may be that the study of economic demography lies within an academic "no-man's land" between several recognized disciplines but not wholly within any one. Most research goes on well within the recognized bounds of the various fields and there is usually relatively little cultivation of the peripheral areas in-between. Yet there can be little doubt that for the analysis of some problems theories which go beyond the conventional bounds of any given discipline are necessary.

1

In this light consider for a moment the problem of the
economic development of the so-called under-developed areas. If we
wish to account for the influence of potential population growth in our
analysis then we must consider simultaneously two factors. These
are: (1) the extent to which potential economic changes will affect
certain demographic rates and the consequent changes in the composition and size of the population; and (2) the extent to which the changing
size and composition of the population will affect the economic state
of the system and the rate of economic development. But to answer
these questions the empirical researcher would be hard put to find an
adequate theoretical framework to guide him in his work. This in-
adequacy is noted by Penrose in his Population Theories and Their
Application.[1] It would therefore appear that there is some need for
additional theoretical work on the subject.

One of the strange aspects of the theoretical work in
population is that the development appears to have been somewhat
lopsided. Although there has been a great deal of writing and discussion on the Malthusian doctrines, it appears that there has not
been any considerable advance in the refinement of concepts or the
extension of the theory beyond Malthus' concise final version of the
theory as expounded in his Encyclopaedia Britannica[2] article. Optimum population theory appears to have had a similar fate. More recent formulations do not go very much beyond the original formulations
by Cannan and Wicksell. Yet, in other aspects of population studies,
especially the mathematical-statistical aspects of pure demography, a
great deal of progress has been made, much of it due to the pioneer
work of the late A. J. Lotka. Thus, while in some areas we have almost unduly refined statistical concepts, there has been a negligible
amount of conceptualization of those aspects of the problem which deal
with the interaction of population changes and economic conditions. In
this study an attempt will be made to take some steps toward remedying
this deficiency.

The Scope of This Study

One of the most significant facts of economics and the

---

[1] Stanford University, California: Food Research Institute. 1934, p. 3.

[2] Encyclopaedia Britannica, Supplement to the Fifth Edition, "Population," pp. 307 ff.

other social sciences is mutual interdepence. Because of this characteristic of economic and social phenomena it is never possible to deal
with all of the factors that may enter into a given situation in the construction of a theoretical model. Even an attempt to treat a large
number of the variables and parameters which can conceivably have
some bearing on demographic or economic phenomena becomes exceedingly complex. It is therefore necessary in the early stages of
theoretical work to select certain basic variables and to attempt to
construct theoretical models on the basis of these alone as an early
approximation to more complex theories. In view of these considerations no attempt can be made in this study to give an exhaustive or
complete treatment of the subjects considered. What will be attempted is the consideration of a few central aspects of what may be looked
upon as a theory of demographic-economic development. But the
writer likes to believe that the choice of aspects to be treated is not
entirely arbitrary. First, the various aspects considered are to a
greater or lesser degree related to each other. Second, an attempt
is made in the later chapters to build upon the findings of the earlier
ones.

The central problem underlying much of this study is
the exploration of the conditions which are necessary in order to
achieve a transition from what may be characterized -- for want of a
better term -- as Malthusian conditions to non-Malthusian conditions;
that is to say, the transition from a condition of high birth rates, low
expectation of life at birth and low levels of average income to a state
of relatively low birth rates, relatively high expectation of life at birth,
and relatively high levels of average income. It is hoped that the extension and refinement of some of the existing notions, as well as the
construction of some new concepts and theoretical models, may help to
clarify thinking on some aspects of this important question.

The sequence of chapters and topics follows a rough
logical order. For the most part the sequence is from more aggregative to less aggregative models, and from more restrictive to less
restrictive hypotheses. Thus, first a static Malthusian model is presented; second, a simple macro-dynamic model is considered, and then
various modifications of this model are discussed; third, the possibility
of working with less aggregative models is looked into through a

consideration of the elements of a multi-sector model; and fourth, the relationships between less aggregative and more aggregative models are treated.

Now, in building theoretical models it is often desirable to build upon the work of the past. It happens that a reformulated Malthusian type of model serves as an excellent foundation for the problem at hand. The model presented is a self-contained static system. An attempt is made to state in detail the equilibrium conditions of the model. It will also be shown that the equilibrium conditions can be stated on the basis of two overriding concepts that subsume the more detailed equilibrium conditions. Such a model may perhaps be looked upon as a rough approximation to the conditions that exist in some of the under-developed areas.

Describing the equilibrium conditions of a system is only a beginning. We are usually also interested in knowing the stability or instability of such a state of affairs. In contrast to economic theory, where the interest usually lies in discovering the stability conditions of the system, our major concern will be the discovery of the conditions under which near-Malthusian states are unstable. It is generally accepted that Malthusian equilibrium is an undesirable state of affairs. Much of the impetus for the industrial development of the so-called under-developed areas arises from a desire to escape from Malthusian conditions. We therefore have a pragmatic incentive for the consideration of the kind of displacements from equilibrium that are necessary in order to achieve a demographic and economic state which does not lead to a reversion to Malthusian conditions.

Finally, toward the end of this study the notion of an optimum population comes in for consideration. It is argued that the problems considered in optimum population theory have been inadequately formulated and, as a consequence, an attempt is made to reformulate the central problems that are involved. Among the matters considered are the sense in which the notion of an optimum population is meaningful, the relationship of such a concept to such questions as displacements from equilibrium, and the kind of collective action necessary to achieve desirable kinds of displacements.

Some Remarks on Methodology

The question may be raised whether useful theories can

be formulated at this stage of research. No final answer can be given
to such a question but there are several points worthy of note that are
relevant. First, there is the by now almost trite observation that in
an important sense scientific research without theory is unthinkable.
The theory is either made explicit or it is implicit in the methods of
research. As Myrdal points out, "Scientific facts do not exist per se,
waiting for scientists to discover them. A scientific fact is a construction abstracted out of a complex and interwoven reality by means of
arbitrary definitions and classifications."[3] And it is usually accepted
that there is some use in making explicit the complex of related definitions, classifications, and hypotheses which give potential facts
their meaning. For in this sense, and others, complicated theories
precede empirical research.

There is at this time another ground for theory construction or model building. We know many of the factors that influence economic development and demographic change. Lists of such
factors can be made.[4] However, lists of factors are not theories.
Such lists are only the merest beginnings of understanding the processes we are interested in. It is important to know how these factors
are related to each other; hence the need for constructing systems of
interrelated hypotheses or models.

An obvious methodological point which is sometimes
overlooked is that the objective of theory construction is not the formulation of a body of unquestionable truth. Rather, one of the primary
objectives of theory construction is the careful formulation of a set
of interrelated ideas from which it is possible to deduce meaningful
theorems, by which we mean simply a body of conceivably refutable
propositions. Whether the propositions turn out to be true or false is
a different matter. The determination of the truth or falsity of such
propositions is properly the area of empirical research. The "theory

---

[3] Gunnar Myrdal, An American Dilemma. New York, London: Harper
and Bros. [1944], p. 1057.

[4] For a list of twenty such factors see J. J. Spengler, "Economic
Factors in the Development of Densely Populated Areas," Proceedings of the American Philosophical Society, Vol. 95, No. 1 (February
13, 1951), pp. 21-24.

tester" may or may not be the same individual as the theorist, but
the two types of activity are clearly separate in principle.

What follows, therefore, cannot in any way add to the
stock of factual knowledge in the sense of additional empirical or historical information. All that can be hoped for is that this essay may
lead to one or more non-trivial theorems or propositions that can be
put in such form as to be conceivably falsifiable by empirical research.
This, of course, does not exhaust the possible utility of either new concepts or new theories.

Concepts may be of value even though they are not in-
corporated into theoretical models. They may direct attention to
important ideas that may not have been seen in a fruitful light before.
Some concepts may in themselves prove to be inadequate, but because
they are developed, they may suggest questions that lead to the formulation of other concepts which are adequate. Yet, in the final analysis, the most useful concepts are probably those which eventually get
into fruitful theories either in their original or modified form.

What has been said about concepts holds in large part
also for theories. A theory need not be correct to be useful. An
incorrect theory may be exceedingly valuable in that the questions
and considerations it raises lead to a theory that is correct. Or, less
adequate theories may lead to more adequate ones. On the other hand,
a certain theoretical formulation may really prove to be a false start.
But even false starts may be useful in that they may prevent others
from making similar false starts. The difficulty with much of this is,
of course, that one never really knows at the outset how it will all
turn out.

Finally, a word to the reader is in order. It has already been indicated that simplified models based on more restrictive
assumptions are treated before somewhat more complicated models
based on less restrictive assumptions. As a consequence, necessary
qualifications and modifications of various propositions are not made
at the same time that the propositions are made. The reader will
therefore find that what he may consider significant omissions or
modifications are taken up a number of pages, or sometimes chapters,
after the initial notions that require qualifications are introduced.
This is really inevitable since in expounding a system of interrelated

ideas it is impossible to say everything at once, and hence some qualifications and additional considerations must come after the introduction of the major ideas presented.

CHAPTER II

THE NATURE AND CONDITIONS OF
MALTHUSIAN EQUILIBRIUM

Introduction

In the pages that follow an attempt is made to set
forth, in modern economic terminology, a system of interrelationships that describe the nature of an economy characterized by a high
birth rate, high death rate, low average income equilibrium. The
model presented is Malthusian in the sense that it describes conditions somewhat similar to those Malthus envisioned. However, no
attempt is made to stick to the details of the original theory. Indeed,
such an attempt would defeat one of the purposes of this chapter. In
Malthus' version of the theory dynamics are not clearly separated
from statics, and processes of adjustment are not separated from the
description of equilibrium conditions. In this chapter an attempt is
made to distinguish these separate aspects of the model.

Although the simplicity and determinateness of the
model is due to the simple nature of the underlying postulates, the
model nevertheless permits us to observe some of the basic interrelationships between demographic and economic variables. An analysis of this model serves as a convenient instrument for the introduction and examination of certain basic notions which, with possible additions and qualifications, may be useful in more complex models. Of
greater import is the fact that so-called Malthusian conditions do, to
some extent, have their counterpart in the real world, and hence the
model may prove to be something more than merely a speculative ex-
ercise. Last, but not least, the stability conditions of the Malthusian
model, or of a variant of such a model, have not, as far as the writer
is aware, been examined to any great extent, and therefore something

useful may be said along these lines.

It should be noted that we shall not concern ourselves
with the effects of population changes on the level of employment.
For present purposes it is convenient to chain the Keynesian devil in
order to better focus our attention on the Malthusian one.

The Real-Income Functions

(1) Income and resources. The model presented is
built around three major variables: income, resources, and population.
The definition of population is left for the next section, but a few remarks on the definitions of income and resources are in order at this
juncture. It would take us too far afield to go into a detailed discussion
on the meaning, definition, and measurement of income and resources.
All that can be done within the bounds of the subject matter with which
we are primarily concerned is to indicate the sense in which the terms
are employed in this essay.

The concept of income is used in the same sense in
which Keynes and Hicks used it. We can regard income in at least two
ways. Income is equal to the value of the sum of the consumption goods
and services and capital goods and services produced during the
period. Or income can be defined as the maximum amount of goods
and services that an economy can "use up" (either in consumption of
the goods and/or in depreciation and destruction of these goods)
during the period without forcing the productive capacity of the economy below what it was at the beginning of the period.[1]

At times a distinction is made between what is conceived of as man-made resources and natural resources. No such distinction is made here. The terms resources and capital are used
interchangeably. By resources we refer not only to natural resources,
but to all resources that are employed for productive purposes. Thus,
resources that are not employed because of technological ignorance
are not resources in an economy in which such knowledge is absent.
Once the necessary knowledge is discovered or learned there is, in
the sense that we are employing the term, an increase in resources.

---

[1] See J. R. Hicks, Value and Capital. Oxford: Clarendon Press,
1946, pp. 176 ff. Also, J. M. Keynes, The General Theory of Employment,
Interest, and Money. New York: Harcourt, Brace and Co., 1936,
Chapter 6.

The discovery of how to use something that was previously not employ-
able in the productive process, and the augmentation of existing kinds
of capital goods both represent increases in resources as far as their
economic effects are concerned. However, the concept of resources
is limited to non-human objects. Increases in man-power are not increases in resources in the sense employed here.

        The problem of the measurement of resources or capi-
tal is generally recognized as a very difficult one. It involves all
kinds of subtleties. To enter into such matters here would carry much
beyond the scope of this chapter. In order to proceed we must assume
that there is a communicable meaning to the notion of a given amount
of resources or capital that economists can generally accept and work
with. In an economy where there is only one kind of capital goods the
problem essentially disappears, since it is only necessary to multiply
the number of physical units by some unit of value to obtain aggregate
capital. However, in the case where there are many kinds of capital
goods used, we get involved in an index number problem that is in-
soluble in principle, and one that we cannot pretend to investigate and
solve in this paper. There is no alternative but to continue on the
assumption that we can attach an index or value to a heterogeneous
aggregate of resources in order to give a meaningful conception of the
magnitude of such an aggregate.

        (2) The total-real-income function. There does not ex-
ist at present a well worked out theory of the determination of real income. Yet, there are a number of factors that are generally recognized
as being of major significance. For any unit period the dominant factors that determine the level of real income for the economy as a whole
are: (1) the amount of capital (resources) that is available; (2) the
size of the labor force; (3) the state of the arts, i.e. the nature of the
technological information used in the productive processes; (4) the
level of employment; (5) the efficiency and adequacy of commercial
and governmental institutions, e.g. the central banking system; (6)
the nature of business organization, i.e. whether along competitive
or monopolistic lines and whether business is organized in small or
large units; etc.[2] This list could easily be augmented by other factors

_____

[2] Certain significant random factors may enter the picture such as
rainfall, temperature, frost, crop and animal diseases, etc. Thus, a

of lesser significance. For present purposes we have to invoke a ceteris-paribus postulate with respect to all of the factors except resources and labor force. Furthermore, we assume for the time being that the size of the labor force is a constant proportion of the total population, so that increases in population size imply proportionate increases in the size of the labor force.

For the purpose of recreating a simple and manageable Malthusian model let us first consider the broad relationships between real income, population size, and average income. Thus, if we allow determinants (3) and (6) in the previous paragraph to remain constant then total real income depends on population size and resources. If either population or resources is increased then total real income will be increased. However, beyond a certain point, successive increments in population, with resources held constant, or successive increments in resources, with population held constant, will result in diminishing additions to total real income. This is nothing more than the invocation of the classical law of diminishing returns. We assume that for every level of population and resources the maximum output consistent with that level is produced. With resources constant, the operation of diminishing returns will lead to a lower output per head for a larger population. Although it is true that up to a point there may be increasing returns per unit of population, we may safely ignore this portion of the real income-population curve at present since it is not relevant to Malthusian conditions.

A distinction to be kept in mind throughout is that of a movement along a curve and a shift in the curve itself. For example, we can visualize a real income-population curve on a graph in which the level of real income is shown on the ordinate and population size on the abscissa. Now, an increase in population is represented by a movement along the curve, but an increase in resources is represented by a shift in the curve upward. Generally, an increase in resources, with population fixed, will result in an increase in total output. It can certainly never result in less total output than before since, at worst, the economy can always use the old quantity of resources and be no

---

more accurate way of viewing the situation would be to conceive of a certain mathematical expectation of some level of real income resulting from a given constellation of the factors considered above.

worse off than before. Of course, between any two points in time changes in both population and resources are likely to take place. Indeed, the simultaneous movements of both resources and population are the pivotal points around which our analysis of stability conditions will revolve.

(3) The average real income function. The function to be considered now is derived from the total real income function.

By average real income we mean simply total real income divided by population size. In symbols the average real income function may be written

$$y = y(P,K) \tag{1}$$

where y denotes average real income, P stands for population size, and K stands for capital or resources. If K is fixed, then y is a monotonic decreasing function of P for the portion of the curve that we are interested in. This implies the familiar postulate that beyond a point diminishing average returns sets in as laborers are added to the work force. One of the reasons for this is the fact that more laborers, ceteris paribus, implies that each laborer, on the average, has less resources to work with and hence output per head declines as laborers are added. On the other hand, if population is held constant, and resources are added, then each unit of labor has more resources to work with, and as a consequence real income per head increases. Thus, y is a monotonic increasing function of K, if P is fixed.

(4) The "subsistence" income structure. It is sometimes thought that the Malthusian scheme relies on the notion of a subsistence wage. This may be a convenient concept under the assumption that all wage earners receive the same wage. But, under the somewhat more realistic assumption that there is an unequal income distribution, a more convenient concept is that of a "subsistence"[3] income structure.

By an income structure we mean something that is analogous to the notion of an age structure; that is, we refer to the distribution of the population among income groups. To clarify this idea it

----

[3] This term is used for want of a better one. "Subsistence" has some connotations that are not intended in this context.

is necessary to indicate the sense in which the concept of an income group is to be employed here. By an income group we refer to the members of a group characterized by a given position in the income range, and not to a group identified by a given absolute income per head. That is, we conceive of every income earner being characterized by a given position in the income distribution. All individuals characterized by the same position in the income distribution are members of the same income group. If the income range and income distribution remain constant as total and average income fluctuates, then as average income increases individuals in the same income group receive higher absolute incomes, and as average income decreases people in the same income group receive lower absolute incomes.[4] We thus conceive of the range between the lowest and highest incomes divided up into a number of "income positions" that represent points on or equal segments of the income range, each point or segment identified by its proportionate distance (i.e. proportionate to the magnitude of the income range) from the bottom of the income range.

Now, if there is no mobility between income groups then there exists an absolute income level for each group which permits that group to just replace itself. As an example consider the case of the lowest income group. We assert that there is a relationship between the size of the income group and the absolute level of average income enjoyed by the members of that group. Further, there exists an income level that permits the workers in the lowest income group to exist and to replace themselves, but that does not permit these workers to improve their position and/or increase their numbers. At that level the forces of fertility and mortality are such that average family size is just sufficient to replace the people in that group. Higher income levels would permit greater consumption, a diminution in mortality, an increase in births, and hence an increase in numbers; while lower income levels would have the opposite effects. We shall call the income level that permits the lowest group just to replace itself the subsistence wage or income for that group. Similarly, the income structure that

---

[4] We postulate that within any income group the ratio of labor force to the total population of the group is the same as that of the population as a whole.

just permits the entire population to replace itself we shall call the
subsistence income structure.

If there is mobility between income groups then income
groups can be augmented both by births and by a shift from other income groups, and diminished both by death and by a shift of some of
its members to other groups. Under such conditions the subsistence
income structure would be that income structure under which the
shift in numbers to and from each economic group would be exactly
equal to the deficit or surplus of births over deaths.

Savings and Investment

For purposes of the present discussion savings and investment are defined in the Keynesian manner,[5] and are, by definition,
always equal ex post. Net savings for the economy is equal to net
national income minus consumption, and net investment is equal to the
output of goods other than those used in consumption less depreciation
on existing capital. Since we are not concerned with the problem of
changing levels of employment due to monetary inflation or deflation
we assume that there is no hoarding or forced saving in the economy,
and hence intended (ex ante) savings are also equal to investment. In
view of these postulates we can interchange the words savings and investment in what follows without changing the nature of the argument
in any respect.

It is now important to consider the factors that determine the level of net savings and investment since these, in turn, determine the extent to which capital is augmented or diminished within
any period. An exhaustive treatment of this subject is, of course, beyond the scope of this essay. A simple and not unreasonable assumption about the relationship between savings, the level of income, and
the income distribution is adequate for present purposes. We postulate, therefore, that savings (= investment) is a function of the level
of income and the distribution of income, if the interest rate is relatively constant or assumed to be an inconsequential determinant. This
implies that an income distribution skewed toward higher income groups
will yield, ceteris paribus, higher net savings than an income distribu-

---

[5] Keynes, op. cit., Chapters 6 and 7.

tion skewed toward lower income groups. However, in conformity
with recent findings,[6] we make the additional assumption that income
groups accustomed to a higher standard of living have a higher propensity to consume (i.e. a lower propensity to save) than those accustomed to a lower standard. This notion may be made clear by the
following diagram.

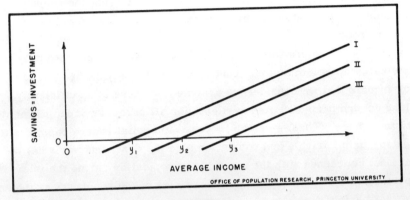

FIGURE 1

In Fig. 1 the curves labeled I, II, and III, represent the savings functions (i.e. the relationship between savings and the average real income for each group) of three income groups (assuming there are only
three income groups in the economy). Now the income distribution remains the same for every level of national income. As average real
income for the entire economy rises, the average income in each group
rises accordingly. The people in group III are in a higher income group
than those in group II, who in turn are in a higher one than those in
group I. Thus, for every level of national income the people in group
III are accustomed to higher average incomes than those in groups I
and II. If average income for each of the three groups is y_1, y_2, and
y_3, respectively, then savings is zero. If average income for each
group is above y_1, y_2, and y_3, then there is net savings, and if average income for each group is below y_1, y_2, and y_3, then there is net
dissavings. We shall see that one of the conditions of equilibrium is

[6] On this point cf. James S. Duesenberry, Income, Saving, and the
Theory of Consumer Behavior. Cambridge: Harvard University Press,
1949, Chapters 2-5.

that net savings for each income group be zero -- but more on this
point later.

The Population Supply Function

We consider at this point two relationships that have to
do with population size. These are: (1) the relationship between population size and total capital or resources (the population-capital
function), and (2) the relationship between population and average real
income (the population supply function). The important relationship
for the model that is being developed is the population supply function.

Since this is a static model we are concerned only with
virtual equilibrium states. That is to say, for any change in capital
or income that we consider we assume that there is a sufficiently
long enough period of time available for all necessary readjustments
to take place. Thus, given an increase in capital (where capital is the
independent variable and population size the dependent variable) we
are not concerned with the sizes of the population during the intervening
period of adjustment but only with the size of the population at the end
of that period.

In symbols the basic functional relationship between
population size and other variables may be written as follows:

$$P = \phi(y, K) \tag{2}$$

where the symbols P, y, and K denote, as before, population size,
average income, and capital, respectively. The nature of the relationship between population size, income, and capital is indicated in Fig.
2. It should be noted, however, that Fig. 2 is meant to be only illustrative. It is not intended as a demonstration of the determination of
virtual equilibrium points. In Fig. 2 the curve marked K_1 represents
the relationship between total income and population on the assumption
that capital remains fixed at K_1. Similarly the curves marked K_2
and K_3 represent the same relationship on the alternate assumptions
that capital is at a level of K_2 and K_3, respectively. The shape of
the curves is convex downward to reflect diminishing returns consequent
upon incremental increases in population.

Let us consider the curve K_1. For every population
size there is a corresponding level of national income on the curve.

Now, the level of national income may be such as to permit the population to increase, or to permit the population just to maintain itself,
or to cause the population to decrease. Clearly, the only level of national income that is consistent with an equilibrium of population and resources is that level which causes population neither to increase nor
decrease, but just to maintain itself. On the curve K_1 there is only

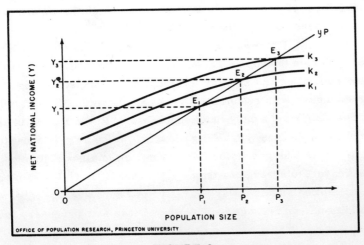

FIGURE 2

one point that will lead to this equilibrium between population and resources. Similarly, on each of the curves K_2 and K_3 there is one
point that represents an equilibrium between population size, resources,
and the consequent national income of a given population size and resource base. By definition population size is in equilibrium when the
rate of population growth is zero. In Fig. 2 the slope of any straight
line drawn from the origin represents a level of average income. Now,
we assume for the time being that the level of average income alone
determines the rate of population growth.[7] Thus, given this postulate,
there is a level of average income at which the rate of population growth
is zero. In Fig. 2 the line whose slope reflects the level of average
income that is associated with a zero rate of population growth is labeled yP. The equilibrium points associated with the three alternate

---

[7] The theory underlying this assertion is taken up in detail in the section below on the underlying dynamics of the population supply function.
Also, the consequences of relaxing this postulate are considered later.

resource levels shown are denoted by E_1, E_2, and E_3, and the related virtual equilibrium population sizes are marked P_1, P_2, and
P_3.[8] Now, the locus of all virtual equilibrium points fall on yP,
since points not on yP fall on a line drawn through the origin whose
slope represents a level of average income that is associated with
either a positive or a negative rate of population growth. Thus, any
point not on yP reflects conditions under which the population size
is in a process of adjustment.

From Fig. 2 and the assumptions underlying it we
readily derive the population supply function; i.e. the relationship between population and average income, where population size is always
in equilibrium with resources. This relationship is illustrated in Fig.
3. The population supply function,[9] labeled P_s in Fig. 3, is simply
the slope of the line yP in Fig. 2, which, of course, is equal to average income. The population supply function is a perfectly elastic curve
with respect to average income (y_0). That is, in Malthusian equilibrium population size is always at the point where average income is y_0.
In addition to an average income of y_0 it is also necessary that the
income structure be what has been designated the subsistence income
structure.

The Equilibrium Position

The nature of Malthusian equilibrium must be clear by
now. However, in order to put together some of the major threads of
the argument it may be well to consider the basic characteristics of
the equilibrium position. This is illustrated in Fig. 3 below. The
curve marked P_s is the population supply function, and the curve
designated by y' is the average income function on the assumption

---

[8] This implies that for every given resource level there exists a combination of population size and national income which, once established, would maintain itself over time.

[9] Whether or not this relationship can properly be called a function is
a matter of definition on which mathematical texts differ. Some re-
serve the term function for single valued functions (one-to-one corres-
pondences) while others use the term function in a broader sense to
include multi-valued relationships. On this cf. R. B. Kershner and L.
B. Wilcox, The Anatomy of Mathematics. New York: Ronald Press,
1950, pp. 52 ff.; and R. Courant, Differential and Integral Calculus.
New York: Nordemann Publishing Co., Inc., 1940, pp. 14-18.

that resources are given, say, at K_1.[10] In symbols, the population
supply function can be written $P = \emptyset(y)$, and the average income function can be written $y = y(P, K_1)$. The equilibrium position is determined by the intersection of the two curves as indicated by E_1 in
Fig. 3. The equilibrium population size is P_1, and the equilibrium
average income is y_0, since P_1 and Y_0 are the only values of the

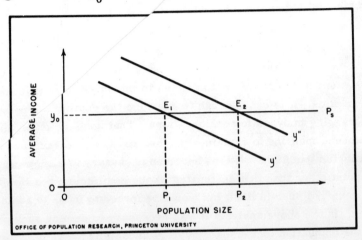

FIGURE 3

variables consistent with the population supply function and the average
income function simultaneously. A population size less than P_1 cannot be an equilibrium value since it would imply an average income
above y_0, in which case population would be growing and be in a process of adjustment. For similar reasons population size greater than
P_1 cannot be an equilibrium value.

The meaning of the notion of an infinitely elastic population supply function can be clarified at this point. Consider what
would happen to population size if somehow an average income above
y_0 were maintained indefinitely. At this sustained level of average
income population size would increase endlessly. This is consistent

---

[10] We may note in passing that Fig. 3 suffers from the same short-
coming as the simultaneous representation of supply and demand curves
in economic theory -- namely, the impossibility of representing the
independent variable of both functions on the same axis. As far as the
author is aware there is no way of getting around this procedure if
this type of graphical method of illustration is employed.

with the moo..n notion of infinity as a never ending process. Thus, an average income a.ove y_0 cannot be an equilibrium value.

Now, if resources were increased to K_2 then the average income curve would s..ift to the right, say to y''. The new equilibrium position under these cir.mstances would be E_2.

Other, more parti..lar, conditions of equilibrium are described at the end of this chapter.

The Underlying Dynam..s of the Population Supply Func..ion

In the above description of the eq..ilibrium position of the system it was convenient at times to introduce ..eas that smacked of dynamics. It is easy enough to describe the equilibr..m points without dragging in dynamic considerations. That done, howeve.., it becomes incumbent upon one to explain why other points are not or cann.t be equilibrium positions. It thus becomes necessary to explain why at any point other than that designated as the equilibrium position the system could not sustain itself but would be forced to move to another position. In the above analysis it was necessary to employ such phrases as "the population increases if average income is above y_0," or "savings would be positive if average income were above a certain level," etc. The point of such remarks was to show that the state of the system would be changing at any but the equilibrium position(s). It is to be noted that such remarks are not properly part of the description of a static model. They are in addition to such a description and answer a different kind of question. They answer the question why certain points do not represent equilibrium states. This is clearly different from the question why certain other points are equilibrium states. Yet the former question is clearly of interest and necessary for a proper understanding of the nature of the model.

In this section an attempt will be made to explain the assumptions underlying the infinitely elastic nature of the population supply function. It turns out that these assumptions are dynamic in character since they explain why points not on the horizontal line P_s (Fig. 3) cannot be part of the population supply function. At the same time, we will be explaining in more detail why points other than E_1 (or E_2 if resources are K_2) in Fig. 3 do not represent equilibrium states of the system.

Explicitly the population supply function is a relationship between population size (the dependent variable) and average income, although implicitly population size is also related to capital,
since the population supply curve, as a locus of virtual equilibrium
points, implies that whatever level of resources is given population
size is in equilibrium with that level of resources. Now it is clear
that one of the equilibrium conditions is that population size has no
tendency to increase or decrease when in equilibrium. To understand the population supply function it may be useful to examine the
relationships between the determinants of population size and average income in a Malthusian type of model. That is to say we shall
specify and examine a set of relationships which, if they existed,
would be consistent with Malthusian equilibrium conditions. This
does not imply, by any means, that the relationships discussed below
do exist at all times and in all circumstances.

(1) Mortality. Generally, it would appear to be reasonable to postulate that the age-specific death rate of a group depends
on the incomes of the members of the group, and on the roles that they
are in; that is, on the things that they do. Thus in a given occupation,
if all the people in that occupation receive the same income, we would
expect that the age-specific mortality rates would decrease if income
increases -- assuming that it is a genuine increase and not a case
where the laborers have to exert themselves much harder to achieve
the higher wage. The reason for this is that at the higher income they
could certainly live as well as at the lower one, and hence there is
certainly no reason for age-specific mortality rates to increase. But
at the higher wage they can enjoy more food, better medical care,
improved housing, etc., than at the lower one. There is therefore
every reason to believe that under such circumstances malnutrition
and the incidence of disease would decline. There is certainly little
reason to believe the reverse to be true. Of course, other factors
besides average income enter the picture. In more arduous and less
wholesome occupations we would expect age-specific mortality rates
to be higher than in less arduous and more wholesome ones. Also
such factors as wars, infanticide, and plagues make a difference.

Thus the role structure (as well as random events) has to be taken into account to get the total picture. But controlling for these factors in order to isolate the relationship between mortality and average income we may say that age-specific mortality rates are a monotonic decreasing function of average income.[11]

      (2) _Fertility_. For a given age distribution crude birth rates are determined by a number of factors. Some of the factors that immediately come to mind are the following: (1) nuptiality rates, as well as the initial distribution between married and unmarried in the population; (2) the values and rule of selection that determine the extent to which children are wanted, and whether or not birth control practices are employed; (3) the extent of knowledge about and the availability of contraceptive devices; (4) factors determining marriage dissolution rates; (5) the extent of illegitimacy rates; (6) the general level of health; etc. Some of these factors may be affected by changes in average income while others may not be. For example, the average age of marriage may decline with increases in income while the values within marriage that determine whether or not contraceptive means are employed may not change with changes in average income. To understand the total effect of changes in average income on birth rates it is probably necessary to examine the effects of average income on each of the factors that contribute to the birth rate. In general, in the neighborhood of Malthusian equilibrium, we would expect birth rates to be a monotonic increasing (or a monotonic non-decreasing) function of average income. The nature and probable validity of this assertion may be seen from what follows.

      (3) _Some_ _basic_ _determinants_ _of_ _fertility_. The relationships between some of the basic factors that determine the birth rate and changes in average income are, in the last analysis, an empirical question. Our task is to postulate relationships which are not unreasonable and which, at the same time, are consistent with the notion of

---

[11] Random events such as plagues and epidemics may lead to exceptions from this relationship. It may therefore be more accurate to say that the expected value of the mortality rate is a monotonic decreasing function of average income.

Malthusian equilibrium. It is in this light that the following remarks
should be viewed.

Values or mores can be a major determinant of nuptiality rates. The values of an underdeveloped society may be such
that the age of marriage for both sexes is according to custom -- say
puberty for women and eighteen for men. Where values of this sort
are in existence the age distribution will completely determine the
distribution between the married and unmarried roles.

In situations where values are not determining, then
other criteria determine the number marrying in each age group. For
illustrative purposes let us assume that the choice depends entirely
on the action of the males in the society. Broadly speaking, the factors determining choice would indicate whether an individual would
choose the alternative to get married if certain conditions exist, or
the alternative not to get married if other conditions exist. For any
individual in the group these conditions are the pertinent parameters
that determine his choice. That is, we conceive of a particular group
of individuals facing these particular alternatives -- to get married
or not to get married -- and reacting to the parameters that happen
to exist at that time. The problem in any real situation is to identify
the factors which determine an individual's choice, the pertinent parameters, and the individuals facing that particular field of action. Once
these are known the number marrying in each age group can be calculated. Now in such a case some of the economic parameters that might
be relevant may be the income of the individual, his accumulated
savings, or the economic condition of his family. Thus if average income is higher some of the economic barriers to marriage are lower
than otherwise. The conclusion to be drawn from an argument of this
kind is that the proportion of the population that is married in any
period is a monotonic increasing function of average income if the role
structure and age structure are given. Or, at least, this would be the
case for such magnitudes of average income as are in the neighborhood of equilibrium.

It appears that Malthus had somewhat similar notions.
In his Encyclopaedia Britannica article he wrote:

"There is no reason whatever to suppose
that anything besides the difficulty of procuring

in adequate plenty the necessaries of life,
should either indispose this greater number
of persons to marry early, or disable them
from rearing in health the largest families.
But this difficulty would of necessity occur,
and its effect would be either to discourage
early marriages, which would check the
rate of increase by preventing the same proportion of births; or to render the children
unhealthy from bad and insufficient nourish-
ment, which would check the rate of increase
by occasioning a greater proportion of deaths;
or, what is most likely to happen, the rate
of increase would be checked, partly by the
diminution of births, and partly by the increase of mortality."[12]

In a society where illegitimate births are an inconsequential proportion of total births, the average duration of marriage
is likely to be an important determinant of the birth rate. Average
duration of marriage is determined by the average age of marriage
and the average age of marriage dissolutions. We have already argued that both the average age of marriage and the average age of
death are negatively correlated with average income. Therefore, a-
part from marriage dissolutions due to causes other than death, average duration of marriage is positively correlated with average income.

On an a priori basis it appears to be very difficult to say
how dissolutions due to causes other than death are related to changes
in average income. Perhaps changes in average income have no effect on divorce rates and separations. It may be argued however that
in a society close to Malthusian conditions religious and social sanc-
tions against divorce are such as to minimize the significance of
divorce as a cause of marriage dissolutions, and as a consequence
average duration of marriage would be a monotonic increasing function
of average income.

In the Malthusian scheme the illegitimacy rate is either
zero or so small as to be negligible and safely left out of consideration.
This hypothesis may be made on the assumption of the rigid value system in the society, or on some other basis; viz., the wide prevalence
of abortion and contraception in circumstances of unions out of wed-
lock, or because of the presumed infertility of "loose women," or

---

[12] Encyclopaedia Britannica, Supplement to the Fifth Edition, "Population," pp. 314-315.

some other cause. Malthus appears to have had similar notions when
he wrote:

> "The remaining checks of the preventive
> kind, are the sort of intercourse whi ch renders
> some of the women of large towns unprolific;
> a general corruption of morals with regard to
> the sex, which has a similar effect; unnatural
> passions and improper arts to prevent the con-
> sequences of irregular connections."[13]

It is, perhaps, of interest to note that Malthus does not
consider the possibility of the employment of these so-called "improper
arts" to prevent the consequences of regular connections. In any e-
vent we assume that in this model contraception either does not take
place or is not effective within marriage. That is, birth control, in
the sense of the conscious use of contraceptive methods, is not a
factor in determining the birth rate. The values and mores of the
society are such that within marriage there are no significant successful attempts to decrease conception. If we add to this the belief that
higher incomes imply better health, which in turn decrease the mortality of women in the child-bearing ages, then the plausibility of the
posited relationship between birth rates and average income is
strengthened.

Population Components -- A Generalized View
of the Functional Relationships

In the discussion thus far an attempt was made to determine specific relationships between specific variables, e.g. between
nuptiality rates and average income. This procedure has the disad-
vantage of forcing us to make more concrete assumptions than are
really necessary. Fortunately, the problem can be handled on a more
general plane so that the theory need not commit itself to so specific
a set of postulated relationships as those indicated in the previous
section.

Consider for a moment the following illustrative list
of factors that conceivably determine, either directly or indirectly,
the rate at which population changes.

(1) Age-specific birth rates

(2) Age-specific death rates

---

[13] Ibid., p. 317.

(3) Age-specific nuptiality rates

(4) Per capita outlay on medical care

(5) Per capita outlay on food and nutrition

(6) Morbidity rates

(7) Abortion, miscarriages, and infanticide
     rates, etc.

(This list is by no means exhaustive.) Each of these factors may in
some way be related to the average income of the economy. Now
suppose that we had a complete list of this kind which included all of
the factors that affect the rate of population change and, at the same
time, are also related, at least in part, to the level of average income
in the economy. We could divide such a list of factors into two parts;
those factors in which a change directly implies an increase or decrease
in the rate of population change, and those factors which only indirectly determine increases or decreases in the rate of population change.
Let us call the members of the former group population components
and the members of the latter group population determinants. We can
look upon both population components and population determinants as
being either positive or negative. A positive population component
may be defined as one in which an increase implies directly an increase in the rate of population change or vice versa. An increase in
a negative component implies a decrease in the rate of population
change. A population determinant may be defined as a factor which is
functionally related to a population component, and only through this
relationship with the population component does a change in the determinant imply an increase or decrease in the rate of population change.
An increase in a positive population determinant implies an increase
in the rate of population change either because it causes an increase
in a positive population component or a decrease in a negative population component.

For a closed economy the population components are
death rates, birth rates, or subdivisions of death rates and birth rates.
This does not imply that for a model of a closed economy there are
necessarily only two population components to be considered, since it
may be fruitful to subdivide birth rates and/or death rates by some
classificatory device or other. For example, the birth rates of some
groups in an economy may be positively correlated with income while

those of other groups may be negatively correlated with average income. In an open economy immigration and emigration rates must
be included as population components.

The link between population determinants and population components may or may not be immediate. A change in one determinant, say the average age of marriage, may imply immediately
a change in a certain population component, say the birth rate, while
a change in another determinant may imply immediately only a change
in a third determinant which in turn implies a change in a population
component.

Now let us adopt the convention that when we speak of
a population component we mean only a positive component, and that
when we mean a negative component we have to specify that it is negative. Let us also adopt a similar convention with respect to determinants. It follows that if we could in some way translate negative components and determinants into positive ones then we could subsume all
of the factors (except average income) that govern changes in population growth under two concepts; viz., population components and population determinants. This can be accomplished by using the "obverse"
of every negative population component and the obverse of every negative population determinant in our analysis. That is to say, if the negative population component or determinant is stated in terms of a proportion of the total population then the obverse would be one minus that
proportion. For example, survival rates are the obverse of death
rates. If a certain age-specific death rate is .030 then that age-specific survival rate is .970. It is clear from our definitions that the survival rate is a positive rather than a negative population component.
Similar translations can be made from negative into positive population determinants. Having achieved this kind of translation we can speak
henceforth of simply population components to denote all of the population components that happen to be under consideration, and of popula-
lation determinants to denote all of the determinants under consideration.

Let us denote the kth population component by the symbol
π_k Now if each population component is a proportion of the total population at the beginning of the period, then the sum of the population
components will indicate whether the population increases, decreases,
or remains constant during the period. If $\sum_k \pi_k = 1$ then it indicates

that the population remains constant during the period. If $\Sigma_k \pi_k > 1$ then the population will grow during the period, and if $\Sigma_k \pi_k < 1$ the population will decline during the period.

Now consider the simple case where all of the population determinants are monotonic increasing functions of average income up to a point beyond which the determinants are non-decreasing functions of average income. Such a condition implies that all of the population components are, up to some point, monotonic increasing functions of average income. Thus, the sum of the population components, or the rate of population change, is a monotonic increasing function of average income, up to a point. If the range of the monotonic increasing portion of the function $\Sigma_k \pi_k = \phi_k(y)$, (where y is average income), is from some point at which $\Sigma_k \pi_k < 1$ to a point at which $\Sigma_k \pi_k > 1$, then we have a sufficient condition to explain the shape of the population supply function. Only at one level of average income would the population be stationary (i.e. $\Sigma_k \pi_k = 1$); at any other level the population would be either increasing or decreasing.

The above assumption is more restrictive than need be. It is not necessary that all of the population determinants be monotonic increasing functions of average income. Some of the determinants may be decreasing functions of average income. It is necessary, however, that the effect of the determinants which are decreasing functions of average income do not dominate the total effect of all of the determinants on the sum of the population components. The final result is still that the rate of population change is a monotonic increasing function of average income, but the underlying postulates are weaker than those stated in the previous paragraph.

A few remarks about the relationship between the population components and the population supply function are now in order. The population supply function is static in nature. It does not tell us anything about how population reacts to new conditions. On the other hand, the relationship between the population components and average income do tell us something about the way population size reacts to new economic conditions. The sum of the population components tells us the rate at which population size changes. Returning to our illustration in Fig. 3 we see that y_0 must be that average income at which the sum of the population components is unity. At a level of average

income above y_0 the population must be an increasing one. If the
system is stable then an increasing population will have a depressing
effect on average income. Hence the population will increase at a decreasing rate until the rate of increase is zero at average income of
y_0. The reverse process will occur if initially average income is below y_0 (and if the system is stable).[14] Now more than one population
size is consistent with an average income of y_0. More accurately,
for every level of resources there is a population size that is consistent with y_0; hence the shape of the population supply function.

         The question may be raised whether the population
supply curve is necessarily a horizontal line as shown in Fig. 3. That
depends on the relationship between the level of resources and the
population components. Every point on the population supply curve
P_s reflects a different level of resources. If, given a constant average income of y, the level of resources had no effect on the magnitude
of the population components then P_s must be a horizontal straight
line. But it is conceivable that the level of resources may affect the
population components in some way. Greater resources may imply a
different composition of resources than otherwise, which may be related to a different occupational structure, which in turn may induce
a slight change in mortality or fertility or both. If greater resources
lead to an increase in the sum of the population components then the
P_s curve will slope downward, but if greater resources induce a decrease in the sum of the population components then the P_s curve will
slope upward. Thus, the P_s curve may not be perfectly horizontal.
But the level of resources, apart from its effect on average income,
is not likely to have a significant effect on the sum of the population
components. Surely, the level of average income is much more significant in determining birth rates and death rates than the fact that
people live in an environment where there are somewhat more people
and more resources than where there are somewhat less people and
less resources. There is no reason to believe that a change in the
level of resources, average income being given, would affect all the
population components in the same direction. Such a change may induce a slight increase in some of the components and a slight decrease

----

[14] The whole question of stability is examined in detail in Chapters
IV, V, and VI.

in some of the others, so that the net effect would be negligible. On
the whole it would appear to be reasonable to postulate that the population supply curve is approximately horizontal.

However, the possibility of a positively or negatively
sloping population supply curve must be admitted. As an example
let us consider some of the possible reasons for a positively sloping
population supply curve occurring. Greater resources may mean a
distribution of labor that induces a decline in fertility without changing
mortality rates to any considerable extent. This may come about as
follows: All resources cannot increase proportionately. For example,
arable land or mineral resources may be relatively fixed. As resources increase some must increase faster than others. A different distribution of resources will lead to a different distribution of
productive activities on the part of the labor force. Different productive activities lead to different patterns of living for some, which in
turn may lead to different fertility rates. This last may occur because (1) the change in productive activities keeps workers away from
the home, or (2) the age of marriage may have increased because new
work habits and requirements lead to a different time period before
males feel they are financially ready for marriage, or (3) a change in
the urban-rural distribution may lead to some slight change in values
or mores, or in the adherence to existing values or mores, so that the
desire for children declines and crude methods of birth control are
employed. These are merely a representative group of possible reasons.
But, whatever the reasons, it is conceivable that fertility may change
even though average income does not change but the distribution of
capital and productive activities does.

This model may, if we wish, be complicated further by
introducing secular movements in fertility and mortality. That is to
say, we can superimpose on the model exogenous movements in mortality and fertility rates that are not related directly to changes in
average income. For example, there may be a secular reduction in
mortality due to the application of the discoveries in medicine and public health. Such declines in mortality would be illustrated by downward shifts in the population supply function in Fig. 3. On the other
hand the spread of new ideas may conceivably lead to such changes in
mores and in marital and reproductive practices that fertility rates

fall. Such changes, other things equal, would be reflected by an upward shift in the population supply function. Usually, secular declines
in mortality are likely to precede and be more significant than secular declines in fertility.[15] This implies, all things considered, that
in some cases there is a strong likelihood of a secular downward
movement in the population supply function.

Although it may be argued that incorporating such secular movements into the model would make it more realistic, this will
not be done at present. The reason for this is that the present equilibrium model, which is to be used as a basis for the dynamic models
to be developed in the ensuing chapters, would be made needlessly
complex without changing the results in any significant way. There
would appear to be no point in adding to the problems of exposition if
little is to be gained thereby.

The Equilibrium Conditions

A summary of the major conditions of Malthusian equilibrium follows:

(1) The average income of the economy and the distribution of income within the economy must be such that there is no
tendency at that level for either population size or resources to increase or decrease. The income structure must be equal to what has
been called the subsistence income structure; that is, the income structure must be one that induces neither increases nor decreases in the
numbers of any income group.

(2) The "subsistence" average income must be identi-
cal with the level of average income at which net savings and investment are zero. Otherwise, there will be an augmentation or depletion
of resources, a temporary increase or decrease in average income and
a change in population size. This does not imply that the process of
saving does not go on in such an economy. It implies only that the
saving of some is exactly equal to the dissaving of others. However,
the aggregate debt structure must remain constant over time, since a
change in the debt structure implies a change in income distribution

---

[15] Cf. Frank W. Notestein, "Population -- The Long View," in Food
for the World (T. W. Schultz, ed.). Chicago: University of Chicago
Press, 1945, pp. 36 ff.

via changes in the structure of interest payments.

(3) The level and structure of interest rates must be such as to induce neither net savings nor net dissavings for the economy as a whole.

(4) For any given level of resources the population size must be such that resources per head will yield an income per head just sufficient to sustain the population.

The following equilibrium conditions are of a demographic nature. They indicate some of the conditions necessary for the size and composition of the population to remain constant through time.

(5) Total births must equal total deaths.[16]

(6) Age-specific fertility rates and age-specific mortality rates must remain constant period after period so that the age composition remains the same.

(7) Aggregate marriages must equal aggregate dissolutions. Age-specific nuptiality rates and age-specific dissolution rates (from all causes) must be constant over time. This permits the average duration of marriage and the birth rate to be the same period after period.

(8) The rate of those entering each occupational group in the labor force must equal the rate of those leaving each occupational group. This permits the occupational structure to remain constant over time.

All of this has the appearance of Professor Viner's balanced aquarium idea of equilibrium.[17] While within the system there is activity and motion, this activity is so synchronized that the state of the system is the same period after period.

It may be of interest to note that one of the characteristics of Malthusian equilibrium is that, at equilibrium, the major variables are at their extreme values consistent with the survival of the population. For example, at equilibrium, (1) population size is at a maximum consistent with given resources, technology, and the

---

[16] We assume throughout a closed economy.

[17] Suggested by Prof. Jacob Viner in his graduate course at Princeton University, spring term, 1948.

organization of the economy; (2) average income is at a minimum consistent with the survival of the population; (3) birth rates and death
rates are both at a maximum consistent with survival of the population. Of course, at equilibrium, neither is average income at the absolute minimum possible nor is the mortality rate at the maximum
possible. However, lower average incomes and higher mortality rates,
if sustained, would lead to the eventual extinction of the population.

CHAPTER III

DISPLACEMENTS, STATICS, DYNAMICS, AND
INSTABILITY

The Complementarity Between Statics and Dynamics

A static analysis explains or describes the nature and
state of a system when that system is at rest. In real situations, however, we rarely, if ever, encounter a case in which a system is abso-
lutely in equilibrium -- where the systems we have in mind refer to
those which have something to do with human behavior. We may encounter situations which are so close to equilibrium that an understanding of the equilibrium conditions gives a reasonably adequate
understanding of the actual state in existence. But understanding only
the equilibrium position of a system is, at best, only partial understanding -- equilibrium conditions are only one part of the story. In a world
of flux where displacements from equilibrium are bound to occur we
are also, and at times primarily, interested in understanding the behavior of the system when it is not in equilibrium. More specifically,
with respect to the Malthusian equilibrium described in the last chapter, we would want to know what happens to the magnitudes of the variables of the system if the high fertility, high mortality, low average
income equilibrium position is subjected to a given displacement. Such
a question cannot usually be answered on the basis of static analysis
alone.[1]

---

[1] Quite a bit has been written on the notions of statics and dynamics
in economics. A discussion of these notions can be found in W. C.
Hood, "Some Aspects of the Treatment of Time in Economic Theory,"
The Canadian Journal of Economics and Political Science, Vol. 14, No.
4 (Nov., 1948), pp. 453-468. See also the following: P. A. Samuelson,
Foundations of Economic Analysis. Cambridge: Harvard University
Press, 1947, Chapters 9, 10, and 11; J. M. Clark, Preface to Social

Now, when we speak of a system at "rest" we do not refer to that state of the system in which no activity takes place. Rather, the basic idea of the static state is that of equilibrium -- a state in which there is a balance of forces. As Knight points out[2] the idea of equilibrium as "the mutual cancellation of two or more forces," is an idea social scientists have taken over from mechanics. The concept of forces is perhaps unfortunate because of its vagueness when transferred to the realm of the social sciences. Essentially, what we mean by the notion of equilibrium in economics and demography is a balance of interrelated _processes_ such that these processes repeat themselves with the same intensity period after period. To be more specific in the economic-demographic problems with which we are dealing we are concerned with the balance of such processes as births and deaths, with income creation and consumption, with capital creation and capital depreciation, with the movements in and out of various occupational and social groupings, and so on. Thus, in speaking of equilibrium conditions we have attempted to define the circumstances under which there is continuity of certain stated economic and demographic processes, but under which there is neither growth nor contraction of these processes. Now, as soon as we consider the means or events through which such a balance of processes is established we are in the field of dynamics, and the question of the relationship between statics and dynamics comes to the fore.

The solution to a set of simultaneous equations, in which all the variables refer to the same time period, that describe the position of the system when it is at "rest" cannot tell us anything about the behavior of the variables when the system is in a process of change. Although this point is not always grasped it must be obvious that we

Economics. New York: Farrar and Rinehart, Inc., 1936, pp. 196-228; Frank Knight, The Ethics of Competition, New York: Harper and Brothers, 1935, Chapter 6; J. R. Hicks, Value and Capital. Oxford: Clarendon Press, 1939, pp. 115-127; R. Frisch, "On the Notion of Equilibrium and Disequilibrium," Review of Economic Studies, Vol. 3, No. 2 (Feb., 1936), pp. 100-105; Erik Lindahl, Studies in the Theory of Money and Capital. London: Allen [1939], Part I: "The Dynamic Approach to Economic Theory"; Jan Tinbergen, The Dynamics of Business Cycles. Chicago: University of Chicago Press, 1950, Chapter 9.

[2] Knight, op. cit., pp. 163 ff.

cannot understand how a thing moves merely from what that thing is like when at rest. Therefore, in order to understand the motion of a system we must take into account dynamic considerations; that is to say, ideas or models of the causal sequence of change over time.

Professor Samuelson has argued that the stability of equilibrium can be determined only on the basis of a dynamic analysis, although static considerations are sufficient for the determination of the equilibrium conditions.[3] Whether this assertion is universally true is a question that cannot be examined here.[4] However, as will become evident as we go along, it will be seen that this division of labor between static and dynamic analysis is a convenient approach to the problems here considered. Another way of looking at the matter is that statics and dynamics complement each other. To know something about the nature of the equilibrium position of a system may be of interest, but the extent to which the system will tend to return to the equilibrium position may, from the point of view of many problems, be of much greater interest. Thus, static models which describe the equilibrium positions of a given set of variables and dynamic models which describe the transition paths of the variables from disequilibrium to equilibrium positions, or from one disequilibrium position to another, really give complementary views of the set of interrelationships between the variables. Each view by itself gives an incomplete picture, since both views are necessary for a fuller understanding of the phenomena under consideration.

Now, for our purposes it is neither useful nor convenient to consider the dynamics of a system completely in abstraction. It will be necessary to specify the starting point, or initial state of the system, as well as a description of the causal connection between the ordering of events. If the specified initial state of the system is an equilibrium position then the dynamic model will indicate that the same state of the system will repeat itself every period. On the other hand, if the initial state is a disequilibrium position then the dynamic model will indicate whether the system will return to a former equilibrium state, or whether the system will go to a new equilibrium state (i.e. if

[3] Samuelson, op. cit., pp. 284 ff.

[4] See J. Marschak, "Identity and Stability in Economics: A Survey," Econometrica, Vol. 10, No. 1 (Jan., 1942), pp. 72 ff. on this point.

more than one equilibrium position exists), or whether the system
will continue indefinitely in some direction or oscillate in a certain
manner.

Any event exogenous to the system that causes a shift
in the state of the system is referred to as a displacement or shock.
An equilibrium position is usually considered stable for a given displacement, if that displacement results in an eventual return to the
former equilibrium state. Whether or not the Malthusian equilibrium
described in the last chapter is stable depends on three factors: (1)
the nature of the displacement or shock, (2) the nature of the dynamic
model that we postulate as a description of the motion of the system,
and (3) the values of the parameters of the model. However, the
nature of the stability of equilibrium and of various kinds of displacements and shocks is somewhat more complex than has been indicated
thus far. Therefore, before examining the stability of Malthusian
equilibrium it may be well to classify and identify the major types of
stability and displacements that are possible.

Kinds of Stability and Instability

Professor Samuelson, in his Foundations of Economic
Analysis[5] differentiates between four kinds of stability. The first four
categories below follow his classification. Categories (5) and (6) are
not mentioned by Samuelson but are included here because they are
useful for some aspects of the problem with which we are concerned.

(1) Perfect stability of the first kind. If from any
initial state of the system the variables approach their equilibrium
values in the limit as time becomes infinite then we can say that the
system has perfect stability of the first kind. Perfect stability of the
first kind applies only to equilibria that are non-oscillating in nature.
That is to say, it applies to those cases in which the equilibrium values of the variables are stationary values which sustain themselves
over time once attained. In view of what follows special emphasis is
to be placed on the word any in the definition since it implies that regardless of the size of the displacement from equilibrium the system
will eventually return to its equilibrium state if it possesses perfect
stability.

---

[5] Samuelson, op. cit., pp. 260 ff.

(2) <u>Stability</u> <u>in</u> <u>the</u> <u>small</u> <u>of</u> <u>the</u> <u>first</u> <u>kind</u>. If from initial states of the system that represent <u>small</u> displacements from
equilibrium the variables approach their equilibrium values in the
limit as time becomes infinite then we say that the system has stability in the small of the first kind. We should note that a system that
possesses perfect stability also possesses stability in the small, but
that the reverse proposition is not necessarily true. If a system
possesses only stability in the small but not perfect stability then
there exists a displacement, which we may call the critical displacement size, below which the system is stable and above which it is unstable. In such cases the size of the displacement is crucial in the
determination of the final state of the system after a displacement has
taken place.

(3) <u>Perfect</u> <u>stability</u> <u>of</u> <u>the</u> <u>second</u> <u>kind</u>. The equilibrium of a system may not be a stationary equilibrium but a continually
oscillating one. That is, the values of the variables may oscillate
endlessly around the position of stationary equilibrium. If from <u>any</u>
initial position the variables of the system take on oscillating values
of this kind then we can say that the system has perfect stability of
the second kind.

(4) <u>Stability</u> <u>in</u> <u>the</u> <u>small</u> <u>of</u> <u>the</u> <u>second</u> <u>kind</u>. If only
from <u>small</u> displacements from equilibrium the values of the variables
take on oscillating variations around a stationary equilibrium position
then we say that the system has stability in the small of the second
kind. (The famine and plenty cycle described in the Old Testament
may perhaps be looked upon as an equilibrium of this kind.)

(5) <u>Stability</u> <u>of</u> <u>the</u> <u>third</u> <u>kind</u>. If from any initial state
of the system, the system is subjected to a <u>finite</u> <u>series</u> of successive
displacements, and if after the last displacement the variables of the
system approach their equilibrium values in the limit as time becomes
infinite, we can say that the system has perfect stability of the third
kind. We should note, perhaps, that the kind of displacement considered here has an additional dimension, namely time.

Let us employ the term displacement pattern for any
given series of displacements. Now, it is obvious that there is an infinity of displacement patterns possible. For example, some of the
displacement patterns may be of a kind in which successive displacement

are of increasing size,while in other patterns the successive displacements may be of constant or decreasing size. The time distribution,
number, and average size of the displacements are additional factors
that differentiate possible displacement patterns. In view of the rich
variety of displacement patterns that are conceivable it is not possible
to classify stability of the third kind into the simple dichotomy of perfect stability and stability in the small. For present purposes it is
probably unnecessary to attempt a detailed classification and differentiation between long and short displacement patterns, large and
small ones, those of increasing and those of decreasing size, etc. It
is sufficient to observe that a system may be stable for some displacement patterns and not for others, and that in specific cases it
may be necessary to specify the kinds of patterns for which a system
is stable and those for which it is unstable. It may be of interest to
note that stability of the first kind is essentially a degenerate case of
stability of the third kind.

(6) _Perfect_ stability _and_ partial stability. The criterion
for perfect stability is that after a displacement (or after a series of
displacements) all the variables approach their equilibrium values as
a limit. In some systems it may happen that some of the variables return to their equilibrium values, but not all. We may look upon such
a system as being partially stable. In the following chapters we shall
see that in many cases the Malthusian system is stable with respect
to some variables, for example average income, and unstable with
respect to others, for example population size and capital resources.

Types of Displacements

Although various kinds of displacements have already
been indicated a few general remarks about the relationship between
displacements and stability conditions may still be in order.

The simplest kind of displacement is probably one where
we begin with an equilibrium state, permit or induce a single displacement from equilibrium, and observe whether or not the variables return to their equilibrium values, on the condition that ample time is
allowed for all necessary adjustments to take place, and on the further
condition that the system is not subjected to any shocks during the
adjustment period.

A somewhat different situation is one in which we begin with a system that is not actually in equilibrium but is approaching that state. The system is then subjected to a single displacement from whatever position the system happens to be in. We then observe what happens to the system on the condition that no further arbitrary displacements are permitted. This case is somewhat more realistic than the previous one since real economies are rarely in exact equilibrium but may be in positions that approach equilibrium from some direction.

In a manner similar to the above cases a system can be subjected to a series of successive displacements beginning from either equilibrium or disequilibrium positions. After the final displacement no further arbitrary displacements are permitted, and the ensuing course of the system is observed.

Displacements may be further differentiated with respect to their nature and source. A displacement may cause some of the variables to take on disequilibrium values but not others. It clearly may make a difference to the consequent behavior of the system whether one set or some other set of variables takes on disequilibrium values initially. For example, a displacement whose initial effect is to reduce population size is quite different in its consequences from one whose initial effect is to increase resources. Although the distinction is obvious it is nevertheless vital since a system may be stable for some kinds of displacements but not for others.

The major variables that we shall be concerned with initially are population size, average income, and total capital resources. Let us denote the equilibrium values of these variables by P_0, y_0, and K_0, respectively. By definition, if any displacement (or series of displacements) induces a series of reactions that leads the variables to return to P_0, y_0, and K_0, then the system is perfectly stable. If any displacement that induces an increase (decrease) sets up reactions that cause average income to decrease (increase) then the system is stable with respect to average income, although it may not be stable with respect to some other variable. For example, if the only reactions to an average income above y_0 were increases in population size, which in turn depressed average income, K_0 remaining constant, then clearly the system must be stable with respect

to average income, although it may not be stable with respect to population size. On the other hand, if the only effect of an average income above y_0 was to induce positive net savings and investment,
which in turn increased total income, population size remaining constant, then the system is clearly unstable with respect to both average income and capital resources. But both of these examples are
much too much an oversimplification of reality to be worthy of consideration. The interesting cases are those in which some of the reactions to a displacement induce movements of the variables toward
their equilibrium values, while others simultaneously induce movements of the variables away from their equilibirum values. It is to
models that illustrate such situations that we shall address our attention in the ensuing chapters.

The Significance of Stability Analysis for
Economic-Demographic Problems

The notions of equilibrium, disequilibrium, stability,
and instability do not possess any normative importance, although one
does at times run across passages in both economic and demographic
literature in which the ideas of equilibrium and stability are equated
with desirable states while disequilibrium and instability are interpreted as being undesirable. Yet it is not difficult to find examples in
which, according to some system of values, the reverse is true.
Suppose it can be shown that under certain circumstances a state of
Malthusian equilibrium is stable. Such a state of events might be considered by many as undesirable in view of the fact that it represents
a condition in which the level of living is exceedingly low, and in which
hope for improvement is negligible. On the other hand, an unstable
equilibrium may be deemed to be quite desirable if given displacements
lead to continually rising levels of living. But it is clear that, apart
from a set of ethical norms which evaluates the given states of the system, the mere fact of stability or instability is completely devoid of
normative significance.

Once we become concerned with problems of policy, or
with attempts at inducing improvements in the state of affairs, an analysis of the stability of the system takes on major importance, since the
stability or instability of the system may determine whether any lasting
improvements can be achieved. This can readily be seen from the

following considerations. Given an equilibrium position that is undesirable then it is necessary for the system to be unstable for at
least some displacements if permanent improvements are to be
achieved. This is, of course, only a necessary but not a sufficient
condition. If, on the other hand, the equilibrium position that the system is in is a desirable one, but is unstable, then a random exogenous
shock to the system may result in a movement of the system to a less
desirable position. An analysis similar to the above also holds for
systems in disequilibrium that are evolving toward equilibria that are
desirable but unstable, or undesirable but stable. We need not at this
point consider all the possible combinations of desirable or undesirable
equilibria, stability or instability, etc. It is sufficient to have indicated that the question of stability is related to questions of what is
achievable and ultimately related to questions of policy.

CHAPTER IV

A SIMPLE DYNAMIC MODEL

General Considerations

The highly idealized version of the nature of demographic-economic development described in the ensuing pages cannot be defended either on the grounds of realism or on the grounds
that it may be of immediate utility in the solution of practical problems. The model to be presented can probably be defended only on
the ground that it may suggest the broad nature of the dynamic problem that is involved. The virtue of a good simplified model is that
it can bring out the basic elements of the problem as a whole without, at the outset, getting us bogged down mentally in a complex of
details. Once the basic skeleton of the picture is constructed it becomes somewhat easier to fill in complicated details, to amend certain aspects of the skeletal outline so that it conforms somewhat more
closely to reality, and yet at the same time to preserve a proper
appreciation of the relationships of the dubbed in details and of the
amended parts to the general nature and functioning of the process as
a whole. It is in this light that a highly simplified version of the
demographic-economic process of the mutual interaction of the major
variables is presented.

Simplicity in our model is attained in a number of ways.
First, simplicity is attained by abstracting from factors and forces
which we deem to be outside our sphere of considerations, or which
we consider to be of relatively minor importance to our problem area,
or which are of such a nature that they can be treated and incorpo-
rated more efficiently at a later stage; second, simplicity is attained
by aggregating elements that are not strictly homogeneous; and third,
by postulating relationships between the variables that are of the

43

simplest nature, being careful at the same time not to "assume away" the essence of the problem. With respect to this last point, it is usually recognized that the simplest relationships we can postulate are those that are linear in character. Hence, as a first approxima- tion to a more adequate model, many of the relationships in our model are of a linear nature. However, the basic model presented is not in every respect a linear model since, it will readily be seen from what follows, an assumption of linearity for every functional relationship would contradict some of the equilibrium conditions outlined in Chap- ter II. Toward the end of this chapter, and in later chapters, some of our restrictive assumptions will be relaxed or replaced by weaker assumptions, and the consequences of doing so will be examined.

In view of the general orientation of this essay, our emphasis, for the most part, will be on the determination of the con- ditions for which the system is unstable with respect to average in- come. The major kind of problem to be solved by our simple model is somewhat as follows: Suppose we inject into an economy a given increment of investment; what will happen? The immediate effect will be to raise average income to an amount above the equilibrium level. This increase in average income will induce population to grow and, as a consequence, average income to decline. At the same time the increased average income will lead to some savings and invest- ment which will increase the stock of capital and, as a consequence, raise average income. Thus, our original injection of investment has set two forces at work, one force, that of population increase, causing a decline in average income, and the other force, that of investment out of an average income greater than subsistence, simultaneously causing an increase in average income. Which force will dominate? We shall see that under some circumstances one force will eventually dominate and under some circumstances the other. Our task, then, is to determine under which set of circumstances the average income raising forces dominate the average income depressing forces.

The Postulate of Neutral Investment

Before going into the model proper it is necessary to make clear one of our simplifying assumptions. This assumption has to do with the effect of investment on the population size-average

income relationship.[1] The argument can perhaps best be expounded
with the aid of the following diagram.

In Fig. 4 equilibrium average income, measured along
the ordinate, is equal to OA. The curve labelled F_1 represents the
population size-average income function $P = F(y)$, where P and y
are population size and average income, respectively. The equilibrium population size is OP_1, and the static equilibrium point is indicated by the letter E. Now, the effect of an increment of investment
is to add to the capital resources of the economy, and hence to shift

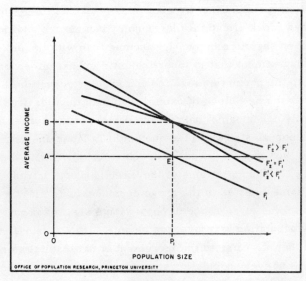

FIGURE 4

the population size-average income function to the right. That is to
say, for every alternate population size labor has, on the average,
more capital to work with and therefore, at every population size,
average income is higher after the addition to the economy's capital
resources than before. However, the negative slope of the new population size-average income curve that results from the injection of
investment need not be the same as the old curve F_1. The relationship of the slope of the new curve to the slope of the old one depends
on the nature of the investment goods produced to augment the

---

[1] Detailed consideration of this matter is taken up in Chapter VI
below.

existing capital resources. The new capital goods may be one of three kinds, which we shall designate, for want of better terms, as neutral capital, labor-elastic capital, and labor-inelastic capital.[2] These three possibilities are illustrated in Fig. 4 by the three curves marked $F_2' = F_1'$, $F_2' > F_1'$, and $F_2' < F_1'$, respectively. The curve marked $F_2' = F_1'$ reflects investment that is neutral in its effect on changes in population size; that is, a given increase in population size would depress average income to the same extent with the new composition of capital resources as it would with the old. $F_2' > F_1'$ represents investment that is labor-elastic in character; that is, with the new stock of capital the economy can absorb additional labor with a lesser sacrifice in average income than with the old. $F_2' < F_1'$ indicates investment that is labor-inelastic in character; that is, additions to the population size force a greater reduction in average income with the new stock of capital than with the old. It is, of course, theoretically conceivable that for one portion of the curve the new curve is labor-elastic while for another it is labor-inelastic. For the time being, however, we need not trouble ourselves with this possibility.

The definitions of the three concepts introduced follow along the same lines as in the above considerations. If at every population size, for a given range of population sizes, the negative slope of the new population size-average income curve is exactly the same as the old then we refer to the increment of new capital as neutral investment. If at every population size, for a given range of population sizes, the negative slope of the new curve is less than the old then we

---

[2] The writer found it quite difficult to find adjectives for the three different types of capital increments that would of themselves suggest the notions illustrated in Fig. 4, and that at the same time would not be too long and hence too cumbersome for ease in exposition. The terms chosen, labor-elastic and labor-inelastic capital, are probably not the best conceivable. They were selected out of a list of other potential designations that, in the writer's opinion, were either more misleading or more cumbersome. As they stand the terms are meant to suggest something like this: By labor-elastic capital we refer to an increment of capital such that the new capital composition permits a "stretching" or expansion of the labor force at a lesser absolute reduction in average income than the old capital composition would permit; while by a labor-inelastic capital increment we refer to an increment such that the new capital composition permits a "stretching" or expansion of the labor force only at a greater absolute reduction in average income than the old capital composition would permit.

refer to the <u>additional</u> capital as labor-elastic investment; but if the
negative slope of the new curve is greater than the old one then we
refer to the <u>addition</u> to capital as labor-inelastic investment. An
analysis of the consequences for demographic-economic development
of having additions to the capital stock which are either labor-elastic
or labor-inelastic in character is left for a later chapter. Throughout this chapter when we speak of investment it is assumed that the
investment is neutral in character, unless specified otherwise.

The Basic Model -- Summary of Symbols Used

Each symbol used in the exposition of the model will
be introduced and explained as that symbol is about to be employed.
However, for ready reference, and in order to facilitate the task of
following the argument, a summary of the symbols to be used, and
their meaning, is presented here:

y_0 = equilibrium average income.

y_t = average income during time period t.

g_t = the difference between actual average income at
time t and equilibrium average income. The symbol is meant to
suggest the gap between actual average income and equilibrium average income; or, in those cases where y_t is above y_0 then g_t indicates the gain in actual average income over its Malthusian equilibrium level.

A = the proportion of g that enters into savings and
investment, or the proportion of the gain in average income that is
invested. Thus Ag is the absolute average investment for the period.

B = the average income-average investment ratio;
more exactly

$$\frac{G_t}{i_{t-1}}$$

C = AB

M = (1 + AB), the g multiplier, i.e., the amount by
which the average income gain above equilibrium is multiplied in
order to obtain g for the next period if population size remains
constant.

r = the rate of population growth between two periods.

m = (r + 1), the population multiplier, or the sum of the population components as described in Chapter II.

u = the absolute amount by which average income decreases as a result of a unit increase in population size.

G_t = the difference between actual average income and equilibrium average income for period t, if population remains the same size as it was in period t - 1.

U_t = the total amount by which average income is depressed in period t due to the increase in population that took place between period t - 1 and period t.

s = average savings for the period.

i = average investment for the period.

P_t = population size during period t. It is important to note that population size is assumed to remain constant within any unit period, and that the growth in population is assumed to take place between two periods. The amount of the population growth between two periods is, of course, equal to the difference between the population size in one period and the population size in the previous period.

Z = the ratio between the initial loss in average income due to population increase and the initial gain in income due to the initial positive displacement. In symbols

$$Z = \frac{rP_1 u}{g_1}$$

The Basic Relationships

The course of average income from period to period is determined, in our model, somewhat as follows, on the basis of a postulated system of functional relationships.

We begin with given capital resources, and a population size-average income function

$$y_t = F_t(P_t) \tag{1}$$

for period t. y denotes average income, P denotes population size, and the subscripts indicate the time period for which equation (1) holds. Given the population size P_t the magnitude of average income y_t is determined. Now, by definition,

(2) $g_t = y_t - y_0$

where y_0 is the equilibrium average income and g_t is the difference between actual average income and equilibrium average income for period t.

The reader should note that g_t is not the gain in average income for period t over the previous period, but is the gain in average income above its Malthusian equilibrium level. This gain of average income above the Malthusian level may have been achieved over a large number of periods. Thus, g_t represents the absolute amount by which average income in period t is greater than the Malthusian equilibrium level. (Of course, g_t can also be negative.) Since we assumed that the Malthusian equilibrium average income is a constant we can always obtain the current average income by adding the Malthusian average income to g_t. Hence in speaking about the course of g_t over time we are essentially speaking at the same time about the course of average income over time since the difference between these two variables is a constant. All of this repeats what has already been said earlier, but since the notion of g_t is basic to the discussion of the model that follows, it is perhaps useful to emphasize the exact meaning of this symbol.

Savings = investment is a function of total income, and average savings and average investment is a function of average income. Since at y_0 savings and investment are equal to zero (Chapter II), it follows that average savings and average investment is a function of g. This relationship can be written

(3) $i_t = f(g_t)$, $i_t = s_t$

where i_t is average investment for period t. Since g_t is given by equations (1) and (2) we determine i_t by equation (3).

The investment of i_t augments the capital resources

available for use so that in period $t + 1$ there are more capital resources if i_t is positive and less capital resources if i_t is negative.
The new capital stock available for use in period $t + 1$ shifts the
population size-average income function to a new position, which we
write $y_{t+1} = F_{t+1}(P_{t+1})$. If average investment is positive, and population remains the same, then g_{t+1} is greater than g_t, since a
larger capital stock, other things being equal, will yield a greater
national income. The reverse is, of course, true if average investment is negative. Let G_{t+1} denote the value of g_{t+1} on the assumption that population size remains the same in period $t + 1$ as in
period t. We can write the relationship between G_{t+1} and g_t as
follows:

$$G_{t+1} = Mg_t \tag{4}$$

where M is a multiplier that relates the difference between average
income and equilibrium income in period t, on the basis of capital
resources in period t, to what that difference $(y_t - y_0)$ would be if
capital resources were as they are in period $t + 1$. (The components
of M are explained in the next section.)

But between period t and period $t + 1$ population does
not remain constant if g_t is either positive or negative. At equilibrium $g_t = 0$, P_t = a constant, but if average income is above equilibrium
then population increases, and if below equilibrium then population decreases. We now write this relationship between the rate of population change and the excess or deficiency of average income over its
equilibrium value as

$$r_t = \phi(g_t) \tag{5}$$

where r_t is the rate of population increase or decrease between
period t and period $t + 1$. We assume for purposes of the present
chapter that r_t is, up to a point, a monotonic increasing function of
g_t. Since $r_t = 0$ when $g_t = 0$, then r_t and g_t must always be alike
in sign. Knowing g_t we determine r_t from equation (5). This permits us to determine the extent of the population increase (or decrease)
between period t and period $t + 1$, which is equal to $P_t r_t$. The population increase (decrease) of $P_t r_t$ depresses (elevates) average

income to a certain extent in period t + 1. Let us write U_{t+1} for
the amount that average income is decreased because of the increase
in population size by $P_t r_t$. (The determinants of U_{t+1} are considered in the next section.)

Combining the results of the above paragraph and equation (4) we determine average income for period t + 1. In symbols
this is

(6) $$g_{t+1} = G_{t+1} - U_{t+1}$$

By following a similar procedure we can determine the course of average income for any number of periods that we please. In order to determine the instability of the system it is necessary to determine the
conditions under which g_t does not tend to zero as t becomes indefinitely large.

The Rate of Population Growth Must Have a Maximum

In the last section we postulated that, up to a point, the
rate of population growth (r) is a monotonic increasing function of
g. We shall now argue that the rate of population growth must have a
maximum so that beyond a certain value of g the rate of population
growth is a maximum. The argument is simple and is based on general knowledge and observation. No matter how large average income
is there must be, for any period, a maximum possible birth rate. This
must be so, if for no other reason than because of such biological constraints as the period of gestation, the infertility of women during
lactation, etc. Similarly, it can be argued that for biological reasons
there is a minimum to which mortality can drop no matter how high
the level of average income. Since fertility has a maximum and mortality a minimum it follows that for every closed economy there exists
a rate of population growth which cannot be exceeded. Thus, if we exclude immigration from our considerations it becomes quite legitimate
to assume the existence of a maximum rate of population growth.

Development of the Basic Difference Equation

In this section an attempt is made to develop an equation that relates the conditions we start out with and the state of the
system in any future period. Or, more generally, we attempt to develop an equation that permits us to deduce how certain given conditions give rise to certain developments over time.

We begin with a system that is in Malthusian equilibrium in period 0. A displacement from equilibrium is achieved by injecting into the economy an increment of capital which results, in the first period, in an increase in average income by g_1. A portion of g_1 is spent on consumption goods and a portion is saved and invested. Let us write A for the proportion of g_1 that is saved and invested. The absolute amount of average investment in the first period is therefore Ag_1. The average stock of capital available for use in the second period has therefore increased by Ag_1. This increase in average capital results in some increase in average income in period 2. Let us write B for the ratio of the increase in average income to the previous period's investment. B is therefore the proportionate increase in average income due to a given increase in the average stock of capital. It follows from this that the increase in average income in period 2 over period 1 (if population does not increase) is ABg_1. If we let M = 1 + AB then we obtain an equation similar to equation (6), which is

$$g_2 = Mg_1 - U_2 \qquad\qquad (7)$$

where the subscripts indicate periods 1 and 2, respectively, and where U_2 is the amount of decrease of average income in period 2 because of increased population size. We can now generalize equation (7) to hold for any two successive time periods by writing

$$g_t = Mg_{t-1} - U_t \qquad\qquad (8)$$

on the assumption that the ratios A and B are constants for all periods. g_t is to be interpreted as the amount by which average income for period t is above average income at its Malthusian equilibrium level.

The extent to which a given increase in population depresses average income depends on (1) the extent of the population increase between two periods, and (2) on the nature of the population size-average income function. For the time being let us assume that the population size-average income function is linear, so that for every unit increase in population size there is a constant decrease in average income. We assume also that an increase or decrease in population size takes place at the point in time between two periods. Now,

let us write u for the amount of the decrease in average income due
to an increase of a unit of population. Therefore, between period
(t-1) and period t the decrease in income consequent upon an increase in population is given by the expression $r_{t-1} \, P_{t-1} \, u$. And, by
way of summary, we have

(9) $U_t = r_{t-1} \, P_{t-1} \, u$

        We are now in a position to investigate, step by step,
the time path of g_t after an injection of a given amount of new capital into an economy in Malthusian equilibrium. Let us suppose, for
the time being, that after the injection of new capital into the economy
the rate of population growth (r) is a constant; that is, we assume
that the rate of population growth is at its maximum. Although this is
true only for values of g above a certain amount, we shall see that
we can develop a useful equation on the basis of a constant r. On the
assumptions developed thus far $U_2 = rP_1 u$.
        Now, the first effect of an increase in capital per capita
is to increase average income in the first period by an amount above
its equilibrium level that is denoted by g_1. For the second period we
have

(10) $g_2 = Mg_1 - rP_1 u$

The right hand side of equation (10) is composed of two terms. The
first term Mg_1 is positive and represents the value of g_2, on the
condition that population size does not change. The second term
$- rP_1 u$ is negative and it denotes the decrease in average income as
a consequence of the actual population growth between periods 1 and
2. Following the same reasoning for period 3 we obtain

(11) $g_3 = Mg_2 - rP_2 u$

Substituting for g_2 the right hand side of equation (10) we get

(12) $g_3 = M^2 g_1 - (MrP_1 u + rP_2 u)$

Similarly, we obtain for period 4

$$g_4 = M^3 g_1 - (M^2 r P_1 u + M r P_2 u + r P_3 u) \tag{13}$$

By induction we can readily see that

$$g_t = M^{t-1} g_1 - (M^{t-2} r P_1 u + M^{t-3} r P_2 u + \ldots + M r P_{t-2} u + r P_{t-1} u) \tag{14}$$

Now, for purposes of analysis it is convenient that equation (14) be in terms of our initial conditions. We therefore substitute $m^{t-1} P_1$ for P_t in (14) and obtain

$$g_t = M^{t-1} g_1 - (M^{t-2} r P_1 u + M^{t-3} r m P_1 u + M^{t-4} r m^2 P_1 u + \ldots +$$
$$\tag{15}$$
$$M r m^{t-3} P_1 u + r m^{t-2} P_1 u)$$

where $m = 1 + r$. Rewriting (15) we get

$$g_t = M^{t-1} g_1 - r P_1 u (M^{t-2} + M^{t-3} m + M^{t-4} m^2 + \ldots + M m^{t-3} + m^{t-2}) \tag{16}$$

Now, the quantity $r P_1 u$ is some proportion of g_1. Let us write Z for that proportion, so that

$$Z = \frac{r P_1 u}{g_1}$$

In words, Z is the ratio between the initial loss in average income due to the population increase between the first and second periods and the initial average income gain due to the positive displacement from equilibrium. We now substitute $Z g_1$ for $r P_1 u$ in equation (16) and obtain

$$g_t = M^{t-1} g_1 - Z g_1 (M^{t-2} + M^{t-3} m + \ldots + M m^{t-3} + m^{t-2}) \tag{17}$$

Rewriting (17) in a more convenient form yields

$$g_t = g_1 \left\{ M^{t-1} - Z \left[M^{t-2} + M^{t-2}(\frac{m}{M}) + M^{t-2}(\frac{m}{M})^2 + \ldots + \right. \right.$$
$$\tag{18}$$
$$\left. \left. M^{t-2}(\frac{m}{M})^{t-3} + M^{t-2}(\frac{m}{M})^{t-2} \right] \right\}$$

It can be seen at once that in equation (18) the expression in braces is the sum of a geometric series. Substituting the sum of the series

$$\frac{m^{t-1} - M^{t-1}}{m - M}$$

for the expression in braces we get

(19) $$g_t = g_1 \left\{ M^{t-1} - Z \left[\frac{m^{t-1} - M^{t-1}}{m - M} \right] \right\}$$

or

(20) $$g_t = g_1 \left\{ M^{t-1} \left[1 + \frac{Z}{m - M} \right] - m^{t-1} \left[\frac{Z}{m - M} \right] \right\}$$

In (20) we have an equation that is in a convenient form for an analysis of the time path of the average income gain (g_t) as t increases indefinitely, for varying magnitudes of the initial displacement (g_1), M, and m. For the sake of convenience in exposition we shall refer to equation (20) as our basic difference equation.

The Time Path of g_t Under Various Assumptions

The results of this section are summarized and illustrated in Fig. 5 below.

(a) With an eye on our basic difference equation let us first consider the case where m > M. The question is, of course, what happens to g_t under these circumstances, as t gets indefinitely large? There are three broad possibilities: (1) g_t declines from the outset and approaches zero as t gets indefinitely large; (2) g_t increases up to a point, and then turns and gradually declines to zero; or (3) g_t increases indefinitely as t gets indefinitely large. If possibilities (1) or (2) should eventuate, then the system is stable with respect to average income; while if possibility (3) should be the one to hold under these conditions, then the system is unstable with respect to average income.

At this point it is perhaps well to recall the meanings of some of the symbols employed. g_1 is the initial increment in average income above equilibrium due to an injection of new capital resources. m is the population multiplier (= 1 + the rate of

population growth), and M is the g multiplier (1 + AB). Now we
know that m and M are greater than unity, and that

$$Z = \frac{rP_1u}{g_1}$$

is positive since g_1 is positive. Given m > M it follows that the
expressions

$$\left(1 + \frac{Z}{m - M}\right)$$

and

$$\left(\frac{Z}{m - M}\right)$$

which are the coefficients of M^{t-1} and $-m^{t-1}$, respectively, are
also positive. As t becomes large the values of M^{t-1} and $-m^{t-1}$
tend to dominate the expression and to determine the value of g_t.
Since m is greater than M the magnitude of $-m^{t-1}$ must eventually
dominate the expression in braces in equation (20) if we permit t to
become large enough. As t gets larger the difference between m^{t-1}
and M^{t-1} also gets larger. Even if the coefficient of $-m^{t-1}$ is a
fraction it must be clear that

$$m^{t-1}\left(\frac{Z}{m - M}\right)$$

gets gradually closer to the value of

$$M^{t-1}\left(1 + \frac{Z}{m - M}\right)$$

as t increases, and that eventually the magnitude of the former expression must overtake and become larger than the latter expression.
It follows therefore that no matter how small the value of Z there
must be a point at which g_t ceases to grow and actually begins to
decline. There must also be a value of t for which g_t is smaller
than g_1. We conclude from this that if m > M then beyond some
value of t the magnitude of g_t must decline as t increases. We
shall show below that under these circumstances g_t will approach
zero as t becomes indefinitely large. Hence, under such circumstances, the system is stable with respect to average income.

The point at which g_t begins to decline depends, in part, on the value of Z. From equation (19) we note that the larger the value of Z the sooner will g_t begin its decline, and vice versa. The smaller the value of Z the longer the period of time before g_t declines as t gets larger. Thus, for any given time period there is a value of Z sufficiently small so that average income increases continually for that period. But the value of Z depends on the value of g_1, since

$$Z = \frac{rP_1 u}{g_1}$$

By increasing g_1 sufficiently we can make Z as small as we please. Thus, the length of time over which average income increases depends on the size of the initial increase in average income, which in turn depends on the size of the injection of new capital into the economy.

Finally, we should note that g_t declines from the outset as t gets larger if $Z > AB$. This can be seen immediately by substituting Zg_1 for $rP_1 u$ and $(1 + AB)$ for M in equation (10). Hence, if the injection of new capital is not sufficiently large to make Z smaller than AB then average income will begin its decline toward equilibrium immediately after the first period.

(b) Now, suppose that M is greater than m. That is, suppose the maximum rate of population growth is smaller than the rate of income growth, what happens then?

In that case the expression

$$\left[\frac{Z}{m - M} \right]$$

is negative and therefore the expression

$$-m^{t-1} \left[\frac{Z}{m - M} \right]$$

is positive. If

$$\left[\frac{Z}{m - M} \right]$$

is less than or equal to one then the expression

$$\left[1 + \frac{Z}{m - M} \right]$$

is positive, in which case the coefficient of g_1 is positive, and hence g_t will increase indefinitely as t gets larger.

However, if

$$\left[\frac{Z}{m - M} \right]$$

is greater than unity, then the expression

$$M^{t-1} \left[1 + \frac{Z}{m - M} \right]$$

is negative, and, since ex hypothesi, $M > m$, the expression

$$M^{t-1} \left[1 + \frac{Z}{m - M} \right]$$

dominates the coefficient of g_1 for all t. We hence deduce from this the important conclusion that for the system to be unstable it is necessary that (a) $M > m$, and (b) that $Z \leq M - m$. This implies that unless the original increment in average income is large enough the system cannot be unstable even under the favorable condition that the income gain multiplier (M) is larger than the population multiplier (m). Furthermore, this also implies that a small injection of new capital may fail to improve living conditions in the long run, while a sufficiently large injection may succeed. Thus, if a program to increase capital resources cannot be carried out on a sufficiently large scale it may not be worth while to attempt to carry out such a program at all.

(c) To complete our analysis we now investigate the case in which $M = m$; that is, the case in which the rate of population growth (r) is just equal to the rate of growth (AB) of the average income gain (g).

From equation (18) we observe that if $\frac{m}{M} = 1$ then our basic difference equation becomes

(21)
$$g_t = g_1 \left[M^{t-1} - Z(t-1)M^{t-2} \right]$$

It follows from (21) that

(22)
$$g_{t+1} = \left[M^t - Z + M^{t-1} \right] g_1$$

Rewriting (22) in a more convenient form we obtain

(23)
$$g_{t+1} = \left[(M - Zt)M^{t-1} \right] g_1$$

Examining equation (23) we note that the coefficient of M^{t-1} gets smaller and smaller as t increases, and that for some value of t the coefficient $(M - Zt)$ is equal to zero. We know also that for average income to increase at all after the first period it is necessary that Z be less than AB, otherwise g_2 will be greater than g_1. If Z < AB then average income rises for a number of periods, but eventually, beginning with some value of t, average income ceases to rise and enters into its steady decline toward its equilibrium value. However, as in the case where m > M, the smaller the value of Z the longer the time before the turning point is reached. As before, this is another way of showing that the larger the initial investment the greater is the initial increase in average income, and the longer the time period during which the average income raising forces dominate the income depressing ones.

The analysis carried out thus far is illustrated and summarized in Fig. 5 below.

The four curves in Fig. 5 illustrate the time path of g_t under the various conditions indicated in the legend. g is measured along the ordinate and time along the abscissa. OM is that value of g above which the population multiplier (m) is a maximum. Thus, above OM the rate of population growth is constant but below that amount it is variable. That is, for values of g less than OM the population multiplier (m) is a monotonic increasing function of g.

Strictly speaking, our analysis is valid only for values of g above OM, since in the derivation of our basic difference equation we assumed a constant population multiplier. However, it must be clear that if the system is unstable, and g_1 is greater than OM, then the above analysis is applicable. Also, it is shown below that if the system is unstable then for some value of t the value of g_t must be larger than OM, and from that point on the above analysis is applicable. Thus, our analysis is adequate to determine the conditions for which the system is unstable.

Consider, for example, case III in Fig. 5, in which $m < M$ and $Z < M - m$. Now, the retarding factor (in our system) to the continual growth of average income is the population multiplier. If m is less than M when m is a maximum, then clearly m must be less than M when m is not a maximum. Further, if g_t continually rises when m is a maximum then g_t must certainly continually increase (as t gets larger) when m is not a maximum. Therefore, if the system is shown to be unstable under the condition that m is always at a maximum then the system is certainly unstable if at some points m is not at a maximum. Case III is especially important since it represents the only condition under which the system is unstable. It remains to be shown, however, that in all other cases the system is stable.

If the system is stable then the time path of g_t takes on one of two general patterns. (1) Either g_t will turn down immediately after the first period and continue its decline until it reaches its equilibrium position at $g = 0$, or (2) g_t will go up for a while, reach a turning point, and then proceed to its equilibrium position. To show that this really happens for all cases in Fig. 5 except case III we have to demonstrate that it is not possible for the time path of g_t to turn up again and continue its ascent, or for g_t to level off at some value between O and OM (excluding $g_t = 0$) either in the ascending or descending phase.

Consider at first the curve I in Fig. 5. Up to time period h average income increases, and beyond period h it declines until the average income gain $(g_t) = OM$ at period q. Now, we have to show that beyond q the curve continues on a path that eventually leads to the equilibrium point at which the average income gain is zero.

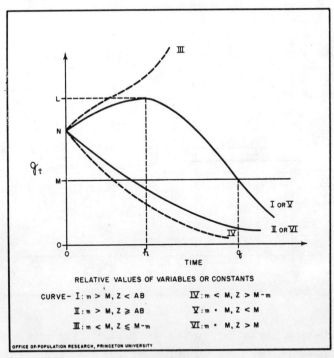

RELATIVE VALUES OF VARIABLES OR CONSTANTS

CURVE— I: $m > M$, $Z < AB$ IV: $m < M$, $Z > M-m$

      II: $m > M$, $Z \geqslant AB$ V: $m \cdot M$, $Z < M$

      III: $m < M$, $Z \leqslant M-m$ VI: $m \cdot M$, $Z > M$

OFFICE OF POPULATION RESEARCH, PRINCETON UNIVERSITY

FIGURE 5

This is done with the aid of Fig. 6 below.

Figure 6 shows only that portion of curve I that is below OM. Can this curve turn up again and continue to rise? Consider the alternative curve I' in Fig. 6. While doing so let us keep in mind our general equation

(24) $$g_{t+1} = Mg_t - r_t P_t u$$

where r_t is the rate of population growth that is consistent with g_t.

As the values of g_t descend from OM the values of r decline. At the same time population size P_t increases period by period. Now, it is conceivable that as g falls from one period to the next, r declines to such an extent that for that period $r_t P_t u$ is less than Mg_t so that the curve I' turns up again. This upward turn is shown at point c in Fig. 6, where the value of g increases from OA to OB. Admitting this rise as a possibility in a discrete period analysis the question is what happens to the value of g now? Can g_t

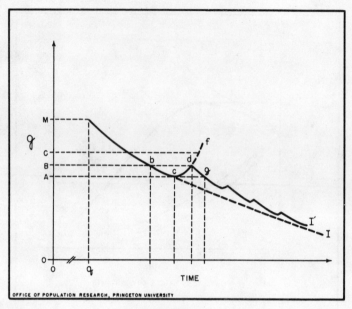

FIGURE 6

continue to rise, say to OC, in the next period? The answer to this
question is clearly no. The curve I' must turn down again at the point
d. If g declines at point b then it must decline to a greater extent
at d. This must be so since at both b and d the value of g_t, and
hence of r, is the same. But population size at d is larger than it
is at b. Therefore the magnitude of rPu at d must be greater than
rPu at b. Since Mg_t is the same at both b and d, and since g_t
declines at b then it must fall to a greater extent at d. Hence, if from
b the value of g falls to OA then from d the value of g must fall
to a point below OA. As long as $g_t > 0$ population size increases as
t gets larger. Since r is a unique function of g_t, and since M is
a constant, it follows that for every g_t less than OM there is eventually a population size for which rPu is greater than Mg_t, and
hence a point at which the curve I' descends to a lower level. Therefore the curve I' must approach $g_t = 0$ as t extends indefinitely.

   We have shown that the curve I' can only turn up for
one period, and that g_t cannot sustain a rise for any two successive
periods once it starts its descent. The apparent possibility of an upward turn in the curve I' is due to the fact that we are employing a

discrete period analysis, and hence precipitous declines in population
growth between two periods appear to be possible. If we choose shorter and shorter unit periods, such precipitous declines in r become
less and less likely, and the magnitudes of the bumps in the curve I'
become smaller and smaller. As shorter unit periods are employed
the curve I' becomes a closer and closer approximation to the curve I.

We now attempt to dispose of the question of whether any
of the curves representing the time path of g_t can level off at some
value of g_t between, but not including, O and OM. The answer to
this question is no. To prove this it is only necessary to show that
for no three successive time periods can g_t have the same value if
average income is above its equilibrium level. Consider the equations for two successive time periods.

(25) $$g_t = Mg_{t-1} - r_{t-1}P_{t-1}u$$

(26) $$g_{t+1} = Mg_t - r_t P_t u$$

Can $g_{t-1} = g_t = g_{t+1}$ when both g and r are greater than zero?
Suppose that $g_{t-1} = g_t = g_{t+1}$. Since $r > 0$ we know that $P_t > P_{t-1}$.
Looking at the right hand sides of equations (25) and (26) we note that
all of the variables are equal to each other except that $P_t > P_{t-1}$.
But if this is so then g_{t+1} must be less than g_t, and hence our
original supposition cannot be true. Therefore g cannot level off to
a constant value and be consistent with our system of equations, except in the case of the system's being in equilibrium and both g_t
and r being equal to zero.

Summary and Conclusions

On the assumption that such things as technical knowledge, economic organizational ability, the nature of government, etc.
are given, then in our model the level of real average income is determined by the magnitude of capital resources per person. Additions to
capital are determined by the extent to which real average income is
above its Malthusian equilibrium level. An equilibrium displacement
that increases average income, the amount of this increase being referred to as the size of the displacement or the initial average income
gain, sets in motion two opposing forces that determine the level of

average income over time. On the one hand a portion of the initial average income gain is invested, resulting in an addition to the total capital stock, which would yield, other things remaining constant, further increases in average real income. The difference between the actual level of average income and its equilibrium level was referred to as the average income gain. On the other hand a level of average income above equilibrium causes a positive rate of population change, which in turn results in a reduction in average capital and hence in a reduction of average income. The absolute size of the population increase between any two periods depends on the population size in the initial period and on the average rate of growth, which in our model is determined by the average income gain. Finally, the diminution in average income caused by the population increase depends on the extent of the population increase and on the nature of the composition of the existing capital and on the size and composition of investment.

Whether a given positive displacement yielding an initial increase in average income results in continuously rising levels of average income or in a return to former conditions depends on the relative magnitudes of certain basic variables. These basic variables are: (a) the initial size of the population; (b) the rate or rates of population growth; (c) the rate at which average income would grow if population remained constant, which in turn is determined by the proportion of the average income gain that is invested and on the ratio between the magnitude of the investment and the addition to average income resulting from investment; (d) the diminution in average income due to a unit increase in population; and (e) the magnitude of the original displacement.

Now, on the basis of the basic difference equation developed above and of the analysis surrounding it we can formulate a series of propositions which summarize the most important conclusions to be deduced from the model. These propositions follow:

1. If the average income gain multiplier (M) is greater than the population multiplier (m) then there exists an initial increase in average income sufficiently large for which the system is unstable. This is not meant to imply that average income can necessarily be raised sufficiently to destabilize the system. Whether the means exist to raise average income to a sufficiently high level to

achieve instability is another kind of question. All that is asserted is that there is some positive displacement from equilibrium average income which, if it were achieved, would permit the system to escape from Malthusian equilibrium. Similarly, if the initial increment in income is a monotonic increasing function of the injection of new capital into the economy, and if M is greater than m, then there is an injection of new capital sufficiently large which, if obtainable, would enable the system to escape from Malthusian conditions.

  2. Even under the favorable conditions in which the average income gain multiplier (M) is greater than the maximum population multiplier there is a critical minimum positive displacement below which the system is stable; i.e. unless the initial increment in average income is sufficiently large the deviations from Malthusian conditions are temporary.

  3. If the maximum rate of population growth is larger than the rate of growth of the average income gain (AB = M - 1) then the system is stable regardless of the size of the initial displacement in average income. Under this condition the system has stability in the large with respect to average income.

  4. For any given positive displacement in average income there is some maximum rate of population growth that is sufficiently low for which, if attained, the system is unstable. Conversely, there is always an average income gain multiplier for which, if attained, the system is unstable for any given displacement in average income.

  5. For any given finite number of periods there is an initial positive displacement in average income which, if attained, is sufficiently large so that for the entire period in view average income continually rises, regardless of the magnitudes of M, m, and u.

  Finally, we may note that in all cases considered the system is unstable with respect to population size, although in some cases the system is stable with respect to average income.

CHAPTER V

DESTABILIZERS AND STABILITY CONDITIONS
FURTHER CONSIDERED

Temporary Fortuitous Increases in Average Income

Thus far in our analysis we have considered only one kind of displacer from equilibrium; namely an exogenous injection of new capital into the economy. In this and the next four sections we consider other possible types of displacers from equilibrium.

First, we consider the effect of a fortuitous increase in average income. Such an increase may come about through very favorable weather conditions during some period, or through a temporary change in the price structure of goods traded between countries, or any other stroke of good fortune that raises the level of average income for some period.

The major difference between this displacer and the one considered previously is the lack of a permanent increase in capital resources initially. Thus, during the second period (i.e. the period after the one during which the initial increase in average income takes place) the productive ability of the economy is back to where it was prior to the first period, except for investment made in period 1 out of g_1. But from period 2 onward the analysis can be carried out as before. Consider the investment made in period 1 as the initial exogenous injection of capital goods. From that point on the analysis and conclusions follow as before. No new principles are involved.

Emigration as a Displacer from Equilibrium

In principle the effect of emigration on the stability of Malthusian equilibrium is no different from any other positive displacer. In practice emigrants usually select themselves in such a

66

manner that there really are some differences worthy of consideration. However, let us take care of this complication later and consider first the simple case in which emigrants do not select themselves in any unique pattern with respect to age, health, or occupational skill.

The first effect of emigration is to decrease population size and to increase capital resources per laborer. If there are no more than proportionate decreases in the absolute number of skilled laborers then average income increases above its equilibrium level by g_1. In principle this is exactly the same as the case in which average income is increased by an injection of new capital into an economy. From this point on the analysis can be carried out as before.

It is sometimes claimed that in areas which approach Malthusian conditions "... emigration can at best but bring temporary relief to the sending countries, and it has been argued that the admission of Indian and Chinese emigrants to the new countries would contribute nothing to the solution of the Chinese and Indian population problem, while it might produce similar conditions in the receiving areas."[1] In our own terminology this is equivalent to saying that emigration leads to displacements from equilibrium which are too small to prevent the system from returning to Malthusian conditions. But it does not follow from this that emigration cannot contribute in any way toward the escape from Malthusian equilibrium. As indicated before, the answer depends on the relative magnitudes of the average income gain multiplier (M) to the maximum population multiplier (m). If M is less than the maximum m then escape from Malthusian equilibrium is not possible. If M is greater than the maximum m then Malthusian equilibrium is not perfectly stable with respect to average income. While a small quantity of emigration results in a g_1 inadequate to achieve instability, presumably there is a quantity of emigration sufficiently large for which Malthusian equilibrium is unstable. In principle, at least, this possibility must be admitted.

There are, however, some differences between emigration and other possible displacers that cannot be ignored. The relative magnitudes of M and m may, in part, be determined by the magnitude and nature of the emigration. Emigration may stimulate and induce

---

[1] Julius Isaac, Economics of Migration. New York: Oxford University Press, 1947, pp. 176-177.

a lower **M** than exogenous investment or innovations. The attitudes, mores, and rules of selection of the populace are not likely to change just because some emigration took place. In a predominantly rural and agricultural country there is no reason to believe that emigration will stimulate new types of activity or new patterns of thought. Investments made out of g_1 and g_2, etc., in this situation, are likely to be agricultural in nature, and possess a relatively lower marginal efficiency of capital, since there is not likely to be very much of an increased demand for agricultural commodities and since the new capital is likely to be of a kind already in use.

On the other hand an exogenous injection of new capital may conceivably be capital of a new type to set up new industries. New industries are likely to have a high efficiency of capital. Furthermore new industries require other industries to service them so that allied types of investment activity are stimulated. Also, the workers left after emigration have to work with a kind of capital structure that was built for a larger population and hence there may be losses in efficiency involved in the necessity of adjusting to the old capital structure; whereas when new capital is injected into an economy increases in population can be anticipated and accounted for. All in all, it would appear that there is some reason for believing, at least in some cases, that emigration leads to a smaller average income gain multiplier (**M**) than other displacers. This conclusion is fortified if the emigration is of a type that is selective of desired economic skills.

At the same time the selection of emigrants may be such as to reduce **m**. If a greater proportion (than in the total population) of the emigrants is in the child bearing age groups than initially **m** would be lower than it would be otherwise. Such emigration would probably also be selective of a greater proportion of the labor force than in the total population. Thus, while emigration initially, and for a time after that, reduces **M** to a lower level than otherwise, it also reduces **m**. Whether **M** is reduced to a greater extent than **m**, or vice versa, is an empirical question. If **m** is reduced to a greater extent than **M**, then g_1 will for a period grow at a faster rate than otherwise (assuming g_1 is sufficiently large to begin with so that it does not immediately begin to decline). Once the effect of the changed age structure on **m** is accounted for the rest of the analysis can be carried out as before.

Some of the general conclusions to be reached from the discussion thus far are as follows:

(1) If M is less than the maximum m, and if the dynamic process is as described earlier in the last chapter, then emigration alone cannot lead to instability.

(2) If M is greater than the maximum m then emigration alone, if sufficiently large, can lead to instability, although the magnitude of the emigration may have to be beyond practical realization.

(3) Both M and m may be, and probably are, determined in part by the type of displacer from equilibrium that is employed. It is probable that emigration leads to lower values of M than other positive displacers, such as the injection of new capital or inventions and innovations.

(4) The cost of achieving a given positive displacement in average income must be taken into account. To achieve a given g_2 it may be less expensive to inject new capital into the economy than to attempt to obtain the requisite amount of emigration.

(5) Finally, it appears that it is not necessarily true that emigration cannot contribute anything to the achievement of a permanent escape from near Malthusian conditions. Emigration, in conjunction with other displacers, may under suitable circumstances result in a sufficiently large aggregate displacement of average income to destabilize the system.

Innovations

The effect of introducing a fruitful invention into the productive process is to increase the productive capacity of an economy's capital resources. For our purposes, therefore, an innovation has the same effect on the values of the variables as an exogenous injection of capital into the economy.   An innovation results in an increase in the value of the capital resources of the economy, and in an initial increase in average income above its equilibrium level. Thus, the analysis of innovations as displacers really presents no new problems of principle.

Compared to other types of displacers innovations may conceivably be more effective for two reasons. First, one innovation may lead to and promote another, or a series of others, so that the

system is subjected to additional "lifts." Second, the intellectual and
social climate which promotes inventiveness and new forms of enter-
prise may be conducive to the reduction of fertility, whereas the exogenous injection of new capital can be imposed on any kind of intellectual and social climate. But it must be admitted that these are
merely possible advantages of innovations as displacers, not necessary ones.

The Cost of Failures to Achieve Instability

At the risk of digressing somewhat from the main trend
of the argument it is of interest to observe that failures to achieve instability may be very costly. First, there is the obvious cost of obtaining the initial positive displacement from equilibrium average income. But there may be more important and more significant costs
involved. The failure will, of course, result in a return of average
income to its former equilibrium level but with a larger population
size. And, if the "bottleneck theory" of increasing magnitudes of u
with increases in population size, described in the next chapter, is
correct, then the magnitudes of u will be larger in the next attempt
to escape from Malthusian equilibrium conditions than they were in the
previous one. Furthermore, every successive attempt to escape from
Malthusian equilibrium must start with a larger population size. This
means that for a given rate of population growth the absolute increases
in population size become continually greater at the same time that
the magnitude of u is increasing. Thus, successive attempts to escape Malthusian conditions face successively more and more difficult
hurdles.

Stability and Instability of the Third Kind

Another way in which instability can be achieved is
through a finite series of successive displacements of appropriate
magnitudes injected at appropriate times. Or, more accurately, this
proposition is true for the kind of model considered in the last chapter
in the case in which M is greater than the maximum m. For this
model the time pattern and magnitude of the successive displacements
will determine whether the system is stable or unstable.

The points to be made in this section can be adequately
demonstrated by considering a series of two positive displacements of
average income as against a single displacement. We assume that the

displacements are achieved through the injection of new capital into
the economy. That is, we assume an initial injection of new capital,
say of magnitude I_1, and at some later date an additional injection
of new capital of I_2 into the economy.[2] What are the consequences of
such successive injections of new capital? The injection of I_1 results
in a displacement of average income from its equilibrium level of
g_1. We consider the case where neither I_1 nor I_2 alone can cause
sufficiently large displacements from average income for the system
to be unstable.

In order to understand the effect of a series of displacements we have to introduce the notion of a minimum displacement
function or curve. We can conceive of a function that relates the minimum displacements from average income necessary for a given combination of average capital resources and population size, the other
equations that describe the system being given. It has already been
indicated in the previous section that for any system there is a critical minimum positive displacement of average income for all values
above which the system is unstable, and for all values below which
the system is stable. (In the case where the system possesses perfect stability of the first kind the minimum critical positive displacement from average income is infinity.) We now generalize this notion
for any set of initial conditions. The nature of the function is illustrated in Fig. 7 below. The curve marked MD is a minimum displacement curve. The point D on the curve MD indicates that if
population size is P_1 then a displacement above equilibirum average
income of OA is necessary for the system to be unstable. The curve
MD is positively inclined due to the fact that as the population gets
larger a greater positive displacement from equilibrium average income is usually required for the system to be unstable.

Now let us return to our example of two successive displacements achieved by injecting new capital of I_1 and I_2 into the
economy. Beginning from an equilibrium level of average income the
first injection of new capital raises average income by an amount less
than OA, say to OB, since we assumed that I_1 cannot cause a large

---

[2] Where I_1, I_2, etc., represent amounts of autonomous investment.

enough displacement for which the system is unstable. The path of
average income after I_1 is one of two kinds. If the magnitude of
MOA is less than rP_1u then average income will begin its decline
toward equilibrium immediately. If the magnitude of MOA is somewhat larger than rP_1u then average income will increase up to some
point and decline. Let us treat the latter possibility first. The path
of g with respect to increases in population size is illustrated by the
curve marked T in Fig. 7. Whether or not the system is unstable for

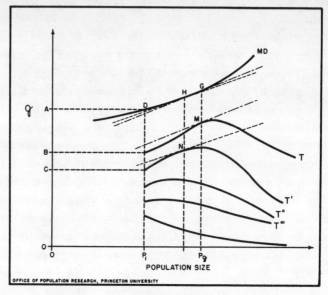

FIGURE 7

both displacements will depend on the magnitude of the next displacement and on the time at which it occurs. To achieve instability with
the smallest additional displacement the displacement would have to
occur at the point where the rate of change in average income with
respect to changes in population was equal to the rate of change in the
minimum displacement with respect to population. This is shown in
Fig. 7 at the point G at which the population size is Pg; that is, at
the point where the slope of the T curve is equal to the slope of the
MD curve.[3] It is obvious that at any other point the distance between

---

[3] In symbols, the point at which the second minimum displacement is
least is the point at which $\frac{dy}{dP} = \frac{dD}{dP}$, where y denotes average income and D the minimum displacement.

the two curves is greater. The size of the second displacement is
MG. It is clear that any displacement less than MG would not lead
to instability. Also, if the first displacement is smaller, say OC,
then the minimum second displacement to achieve instability must be
larger, say NH in Fig. 7. By considering alternative series of two
displacements it is possible to discover the least sum of the two displacements required to achieve instability. This least sum will be at
the point where decrease (increase) in the first displacement is just
equal to the minimum increase (decrease) in the second displacement, if we begin with any initial displacement and gradually decrease
(increase) the first and increase (decrease) the second until the least
sum is reached. It is probably more accurate to consider the least
cost as at a given point in time, say the time when the initial displacement is injected into the economy. It would therefore be necessary
to discount all future displacements back to the initial displacement
at some appropriate rate of discount, before determining the least
sum of two displacements. Also, if the cost of new capital does not
bear a proportionate relationship to the amount by which the new
capital displaces average income then it would be necessary to compute
the least discounted capital cost of two displacements sufficient to
achieve instability, if the cheapest way of achieving instability is to
be determined. However, the analysis need not be limited to a series
of two displacements. The same kind of analysis can be carried out
for any series of finite displacements.

    The question may be raised: What is to be gained by
such a procedure? Why have a series of displacements rather than
one displacement? Three basic considerations are involved. First,
a series of displacements to achieve instability may be less costly
than one large initial displacement. Second, and this is a consideration of some importance, is the fact that a given investment program
may require a certain sequence of activities. That is to say, certain
kinds of investment may have to be made before other kinds can become effective. For example, it may be necessary to build a railway
system before large-scale manufacturing can become effective. Examples of this kind can probably be multiplied. Intuitively, it seems
plausible that a given amount of new capital injected at strategic
points in time may be more productive than the same amount of

capital injected all at once. Third, and this is probably most important, ascertaining the least cost through which instability can be achieved is not the only consideration in determining the best course of action. The cost of alternative displacement patterns must be compared to the discounted value of the average income streams they generate. For example, a series of displacements to achieve instability may be less costly than a single displacement that has the same effect on the stability of the system, but the single displacement may generate a larger discounted average income stream than the series--especially if the desire for increases in present average income is very high, so that the rate of discount for future increases as against present increases is accordingly high.

The conclusions to be reached from this discussion of stability and instability of the third kind are in most respects similar to those reached for stability of the first kind in the model considered. There is however one additional conclusion to be drawn from the above discussion. And that is that there are circumstances under which it may be costly to hurry the injection of new investment (or some other displacer) into the economy, or there may be other circumstances under which it would be costly to postpone such an injection, if the amount of new capital that can be injected is limited in nature. Suppose we have an economy that is in the early stages of development so that average income is at least temporarily rising, then there is a point at which a given injection of new capital will have the maximum effect toward the achievement of instability. For example, in the situation illustrated in Fig. 7, suppose the average income path was as depicted by the curve T. Suppose further that the new capital that can be obtained from outside the system can raise average income only by MG. Then unless the injection is made when the population size is Pg the system will return to Malthusian conditions.[4]

---

[4] This closes our discussion of stability of the third kind. In Chapter III, for the sake of completeness, we also indicated the definition of stability of the second kind. Conceivable cases of stability of the second kind will not be taken up in this essay. It seems unlikely that the kind of regular periodicity involved in stability of the second kind is likely to occur in the real world. Also, the dynamic models considered do not suggest that the systems we are concerned with are likely to have stability of the second kind. For our purposes it does not appear to be worth while to attempt to construct a model that describes a system which has that property.

CHAPTER VI

SOME MODIFICATIONS OF THE SIMPLE
DYNAMIC MODEL

Introduction

Among the ways in which the model described in the last chapter can be amended and expanded are (a) the substitution of other functional relationships for those postulated in the previous model, and (b) allowance for variation in what was assumed to be constant. In this chapter we consider the possibility of doing both of these things with respect to several aspects of the model. First, an attempt will be made to account for the possibility of a declining rate of population growth setting in at some stage of economic development, and second, an examination will be made of the effects of changing propensities to save and invest, varying rates of the effect of population growth on average income, changing income distributions, etc.

Capital Accumulation and Possible Declines in the Rate
of Population Growth

In the previous chapter we postulated that beyond a certain level of the average income gain (g) the rate of population growth was at a maximum; but we did not take into account the possibility that beyond some point this rate might actually decline. Historically, a phenomenon of this kind is what actually took place in Western Europe and North America, and is perhaps what is now taking place in Japan. It is therefore important to consider this aspect of the problem and to inquire to what extent the conclusions of the previous model hold if, above some level of average income, fertility declines enough so that the rate of population growth actually declines. We therefore substitute in the model a new population growth function which differs from

75

the old function in that above some value of average income (and hence the average income gain) the rate of population growth (r) is a monotonic decreasing function of average income. The point at which r is a maximum and the point beyond which r declines need not be the same point. There may conceivably be a range of values of average income for which r is a constant or approximately a constant. We need not consider here the question of whether r goes eventually below zero or not. The problem of a possibly declining population in an advanced highly developed economy is a different kind of problem altogether and need not detain us at this point.

Except for one important point the results are in essence the same as those of the last chapter. For some of the cases we can build upon the conclusions reached thus far.

(a) Consider first the case in which the average income gain multiplier (M) is greater than the maximum population multiplier (m = 1 + r). For this case we know from the previous chapter that there exists a value of g_1 (the initial average income displacement) sufficiently large for which the system is unstable for positive displacements from equilibrium average income. It follows immediately that if the system is unstable in the case in which the population multiplier is a maximum for all values of average income beyond a certain value, then the system is certainly unstable (for certain positive displacements) in the case in which the population multiplier begins to decline after some level of average income is achieved. Of course, if the displacement is not sufficiently large to begin with then average income may not reach the level for which the population multiplier is a maximum, in which case the system is stable. That is to say, for sufficiently small displacements the income depressing factors $rP_{t-1}u$ become, at some point, more significant than the income raising ones. This aspect of the analysis has been considered in great detail in the previous chapter and we need not go over it again.

(b) We now consider the case in which the maximum population multiplier is greater than M. Since the population multiplier falls beyond some value of average income there is a level of average income beyond which $M \geq m$. If average income could in some way or other be made to grow to that point, then we know from the above analysis that at that point there exists a value of g_1

sufficiently large for which the system is unstable. We know also from a proposition developed in the previous chapter that for any given finite number of periods there is always a displacement from average income that is sufficiently large that for any arbitrary finite number of periods which are chosen average income continually rises. Thus, if we choose a period of time long enough there is a value of g_1 large enough to generate an average income beyond which $M \geq m$. It therefore follows that even in the case where the maximum population multiplier is greater than M there exists some large enough initial displacement for which the system is unstable, if population growth is a monotonic decreasing function of average income (or g) beyond some level of average income. Here we have one of the major differences between the conclusions reached in the last chapter and the conclusions reached in this section. The reader will recall that in the model discussed in the previous chapter the system was stable for all displacements from average income in the case where the maximum $m > M$.

Some insight into the problem discussed under case (b) above can perhaps be gained by following a few numerical examples. The details of the examples are presented in an appendix to this chapter but it may be instructive to examine some of their general features.

The postulated population growth function $r = f(g)$ is presented in Table I.[1] It can be seen that up to a point r is a monotonic increasing function of g, and that beyond that point r is a monotonic decreasing function of g. The assumed maximum rate of population growth is 2.4% per period, and hence maximum $m = 1.024$. The assumed value for M is 1.020. We thus have a case where the maximum population multiplier is greater than M. The results of the examples which are summarized in Fig. 8 (page 102) are in conformity with what we would expect on an a priori basis.

From the examples it appears that the magnitude of the initial displacement determines whether the system is stable or unstable. In curves I and II (Fig. 8) the displacements from equilibrium average income are 200 and 215, respectively. For both of these magnitudes the system is stable. At some point the g curves turn down and begin their descent toward their equilibrium values. But for

---
[1] See page 99.

a slightly higher displacement than that used in example II (see curve
II) the system is unstable. In example III the original displacement
from equilibrium average income is 225. The path of g for this displacement is shown by curve III. Somewhere between a displacement
of 215 and 225 there is a critical displacement size for all values below which the system is stable with respect to average income, and
for all values above which the system is unstable.

   The shapes of the three curves that show the paths of
g (and hence average income) on the basis of three alternate displacement assumptions, are in conformity with our general expecta-
tions. In examining the shape of the curves (Fig. 8) it may help if we
keep in mind the general equation

$$g_t = Mg_{t-1} - rP_{t-1}u \qquad\qquad (29)$$

where r is a variable that depends on the value of g_{t-1}. If Mg_1 is
not very large in relation to P_1u then up to a point average income
will increase at a decreasing rate. This is because the coefficient of
u, that is rP_{t-1} is increasing in value as both P_{t-1} and r increase,
while the coefficient of g is a constant. In the neighborhood where
r is a maximum changes in r are likely to be small at first, and hence
increases in P_{t-1} are likely to be more significant than possible decreases in r. The result is a continuation of the declining rate of increase of g_1, that is, if g_1 continues to increase. For these same
reasons, if the system is unstable g will decline at first at an increasing rate since declines in r are at first negligible, and increases
in P_{t-1} significant.

   In the case where the system is unstable (curve III)
there sets in at some point a reversal in the rate of growth. For as
average income grows a value for g is reached beyond which M is
greater than m. At some point the difference between M and m becomes significant enough so that after that point average income increases by larger and larger amounts period by period. Of course,
if Mg_1 is very large in relation to the magnitude of P_1u then the
income depressing factors $rP_{t-1}u$ will be negligible from the outset,
and average income will increase by increasing amounts from the start
as time is extended indefinitely.

The general conclusions that emerge from all this are
in many ways similar to those arrived at in the last chapter. The
similarity in the conclusions can readily be seen from this very brief
summary.

If all of the other factors are given then the value of the
displacement from equilibrium is all important. If the magnitude of
the displacement is very small (in relation to rP_1u) then average
income will begin to decline at the outset and the system is definitely
stable. If the positive displacement is somewhat larger (in relation
to rP_1u) then average income will increase for a while but at a decreasing rate. But the increases in both population size and in the
rate of population will soon be more significant than the constant M,
and as a consequence average income will decline to its equilibrium
value. With a positive displacement sufficiently large that mg_1 is
sufficiently above rP_1u for average income to grow quite a bit beyond the point at which r is a maximum, the system will be unstable,
with average income first increasing by decreasing amounts and then
increasing by increasing amounts as the rate of population growth declines. With the exception of the point noted earlier -- that the system is unstable for sufficiently large displacements even in the case
where the maximum m is greater than M -- the other propositions
derived from the previous model hold for the amended model considered here.

Varying Values of u

In Chapter IV we assumed that the population size-average income function was linear. This enabled us to define u as a
constant and thus avoid a lot of complicated mathematics. But suppose
u is not a constant. The value of u clearly depends on the shape of
the population size-average income curve.[2] (1) If the curve is concave
to the origin then u is clearly a monotonic increasing function of population size. (2) If the curve is convex to the origin then u is a
monotonic decreasing function of population size. Or, (3) for a certain
portion of the curve u may be first one kind of function and then the
other.

It appears that there is really no way of knowing on

-----

[2] As illustrated by the curves F_1 and F_2 in Fig. 4 above.

purely theoretical, or a priori, grounds what the situation really is;
that is, which of these possibilities really manifests itself in any situation. This is an empirical question. If empirical evidence of a determinate nature were available it would be easier to carry out the
analysis since we would not have to consider those situations which
do not hold empirically. However, such is not the case.

We cannot consider all possible shapes of the curve.
What shall be attempted, therefore, is a consideration of the two pure
cases where (1) u is a monotonic increasing function of population
size, and where (2) u is a monotonic decreasing function of population size. There may, however, be good reason to believe that (1) is
the more important case -- purely on intuitive and a priori grounds.
It would generally be agreed that beyond a point there is a limit to
the advantages of specialization. Beyond that point increased crowding on limited resources becomes significant. Furthermore, there is
good reason to suspect that some resources are not infinitely substi-
tutable for others in many processes. That is, in some production
processes an absolute minimum of a certain unit of input per unit of
output is essential. With respect to such resources it may be exceedingly difficult to increase the absolute supply. Such conditions
lead to industries facing successive bottlenecks as attempts are made
to increase the supply of many commodities. The greater the increase
attempted the greater the number of bottlenecks that crop up. If this
argument is valid then it appears that there is at least a portion of
the population size-average income curve for which u is a monotonic
increasing function of population size.

What happens to the conclusions of the above analysis
if u is an increasing function of P? Consider first all the cases in
Fig. 5 other than case III. Under the conditions specified for each
case the system is stable with respect to average income. It follows
immediately that, if under the conditions specified, the system is
stable with a constant u, then the system is certainly stable if u is
a monotonic increasing function of P. For, if g_t = 0 for some value
of t, where u is constant, then g_t will reach zero for a lower value
of t in the case where u begins at the constant rate and increases
as P increases. The reason for this is that rPu, the force that depresses average income each period, increases every period not only

due to increases in P but also due to increases in u.

Now consider case III in Fig. 5.

The effect of a non-constant u on the stability of this case depends on how rapidly u increases as P increases. If u increases in such a way as to approach a maximum as a limit as P increases indefinitely then there is an initial positive displacement of average income sufficiently large for which the system is unstable. For, assume that the limiting value of u is really the constant value, then from proposition 1 (page 64) we know that there is always a positive displacement of average income for which the system is unstable.

Now suppose that u does not approach a limiting value, what then? The rate of increase in u as P increases now becomes all important. Suppose that u increases at a constant rate, say k - 1, as population size increases. Using k - 1 as the rate at which u increases per unit of population increase we rewrite equation (15) to read

$$
(27) \quad g_t = M^{t-1}g_1 - \left[M^{t-2}rP_1u + M^{t-3}rmP_1uk + M^{t-4}rm^2P_1uk^2 + \dots + Mrm^{t-3} + rm^{t-2}P_1uk^{t-2} \right]
$$

and following the procedure employed in the last chapter we obtain

$$
(28) \quad g_t = g_1 \left\{ M^{t-1} \left[1 + \frac{Z}{mk - M} \right] - (mk)^{t-1} \left[\frac{Z}{mk - M} \right] \right\}
$$

Equation (28) is similar in form to equation (20), our basic difference equation. From here on the argument proceeds exactly as before, except that we substitute mk for m, and rk for r every step of the way. Our conclusion, which is similar to the conclusion for case III, Fig. 5, is that if $Z \leq (M - mk)$ then the system is unstable, provided that M = mk.

If u increases at more than a constant rate with respect to P the problem becomes very complex, and its solution is not attempted here. However, a general principle to be deduced from this discussion is quite clear. That is, the greater the rate at which u increases with respect to increases in P, the greater the stability of Malthusian equilibrium.

Equation (28) also permits us to analyze the case where u decreases at a constant rate as P increases. All that need be done is to interpret k in equation (28) as being equal to one minus the rate of decrease in u per unit of population increase. In view of the analogous nature of the results, it appears that there is little point in attempting to restate our analysis and conclusions on the new assumption that k < 1.

The Effects of Labor-Elastic and Labor-Inelastic Investment

Throughout the preceding discussion of the simple dynamic model we assumed that investment was neutral in character. We now consider the consequences of investment (exogenous or endogenous to the system) that is either labor-elastic or labor-inelastic in nature. These considerations are very important because of the bearing of the nature of investment on the magnitude of u.

The terms labor-elastic and labor-inelastic are relative and not absolute concepts. A given unit of investment is labor-elastic or labor-inelastic only with respect to the existing stock of capital. The concepts are meaningless apart from a given stock of capital under consideration. As the concepts have been defined in Chapter IV they say something about the effect of a given increment of investment on the relationship between the productivity obtained with a given capital stock and changes in population size (or labor force). If we write u' for the value of u after the existing capital stock has been augmented by new investment then the investment is characterized as labor-inelastic if

$$\frac{du'}{dP} < \frac{du}{dP}$$

for a given range of values of P, and labor-elastic if

$$\frac{du'}{dP} > \frac{du}{dP}$$

for a given range of values of P.[3]

The effect of labor-elastic or labor-inelastic investment upon the stability of Malthusian equilibrium follows readily from our definition of the concepts. If the system is unstable for any displacements, then a lower minimum displacement is required for the system to be unstable if investment is of the labor-elastic rather than of the neutral or labor-inelastic kind; and conversely, a higher minimum displacement is required in order to make the system unstable if investment is of the labor-inelastic rather than the neutral or labor-elastic kind. The reason for this is simply that u is the stabilizing factor in the system, and the faster u increases as P increases the sooner will average income return to its equilibrium level. The moral to be drawn from this fact is equally clear. A country wishing to escape Malthusian conditions must, other things equal, seek types of investment which are, as far as possible, labor-elastic in character.

Now, one cannot classify kinds of physical goods as either labor-elastic or labor-inelastic. By definition, it is necessary to know the character of the economy into which such goods are injected before an estimate can be made of the nature of the investment. But, given the nature of the economy and composition of the capital stock, then by applying certain criteria (some of which will be considered below) an estimate or intelligent guess may be made as to whether certain new capital goods will turn out to be labor-elastic or labor-inelastic. For example, in an economy under Malthusian conditions in which most of the labor force is devoted to agriculture it is likely that investment that tends to mechanize agriculture, or some portion of agricultural activities, will turn out to be labor-inelastic

---

[3] The classification of new capital (or of innovations) suggested here is somewhat different from that suggested in the existing literature on economic theory. One of the reasons for this is that the existing literature is concerned, for the most part, with the problem of determining the effect of an innovation on income distribution and not with the problem of the effect of population growth on per capita output. Cf. Joan Robinson, "The Classification of Inventions," Review of Economic Studies, Vol. 5, No. 2 (Feb., 1938), pp. 139-142; A. C. Pigou, The Economics of Welfare. London: Macmillan Co., 1938, pp. 674-680; J. R. Hicks, The Theory of Wages. London: Macmillan Co., 1932, pp. 121-122; G. F. Bloom, "Note on Hicks's Theory of Invention," American Economic Review, Vol. 36, No. 1 (March, 1946), pp. 83-96.

in character, while the construction of a transportation system is likely to be labor-elastic in character. The probable reasons for this are
not difficult to imagine. The demand for agricultural commodities is
relatively inelastic. The mechanization of agriculture makes it possible
to produce the same amount of food with much less labor. The demand
for agricultural products is not likely to increase significantly. Therefore, much of the former agricultural labor becomes, in a sense, surplus. Certainly, in circumstances of this sort it will become exceedingly difficult to absorb any additional population on the land. Some of
the former agricultural laborers who are really not needed any more
on the land may be absorbed in other occupations as unskilled labor,
in which case their marginal productivity will be very much lower than
it was before. On the other hand, a transportation system, once built,
is relatively flexible with respect to population increases. More population may conceivably imply a proportionately greater demand for
transportation services. This increase in demand can be met by using
the existing rolling stock more frequently without any marked decreases
in efficiency; indeed, increases in efficiency are even conceivable
under such circumstances. Thus the marginal productivity of the additional labor that is hired may not fall, or fall significantly, in this
case.[4]

The Determinants of the Nature of Investment

We have argued that the nature of a given unit of investment determines, in part, the rate at which u changes as P increases.
This, of course, affects the magnitude of u, which, in turn, determines
the nature of the stability or instability of the system. We now attempt
to go somewhat more deeply into the matter and consider the major
factors that determine the extent to which a given unit of investment
is labor-elastic or -inelastic in character. At the same time we determine some of the more basic determinants of the magnitude of u.

---

[4] The effect of investment on the magnitude of u is not the only consideration that is important. At the same time the income raising
effect of a unit of investment must be considered. A given type of investment may be preferred to another type even if it increases the
magnitude of u to a greater extent than the other if, at the same
time, it raises average income for the existing population much more
significantly than the other one.

The fact that u has a positive value can be attributed
to the phenomenon of diminishing returns as one factor of production
increases while the other remains constant. It is to be noted however
that diminishing returns in this case are not quite the same thing as
the customary static formulation of the law of diminishing returns.[5]
In the usual formulation of the principle of diminishing returns the
situations which are compared are the outputs for alternative larger
units of one input with a constant amount of all other inputs. Working
with alternative units of the variable factor is not quite the same thing
as working with increases in the variable factor of production in a
dynamic context. In the static formulation we assume that larger
amounts of the variable factor work with the same "quantity" of the
fixed factor as smaller amounts of the variable factor would, but not
with the identical fixed factor. The classical example usually cited
is that if we consider a labor force of ditch diggers of eleven men
rather than ten men, the capital in the form of shovels being fixed in
quantity, we do not assume that the eleven men work with ten shovels,
but that they work with eleven smaller shovels which are in some sense
equal in value to the ten larger ones. In other words, we assume such
adaptations in the fixed quantity of capital as are necessary so that
the larger labor force could be as productive as possible with the fixed
quantity of capital. In the purely static analysis this is quite the proper
procedure. In the dynamic case, however -- the case we are concerned with -- it is not legitimate to make such an assumption since it is
absurd to assume that, in our dynamic context, when there are additions to the labor force there is sufficient time and opportunity to re-
fashion the capital structure so that the larger labor force is most
perfectly adapted to the existing fixed quantity of capital.

There are two factors which, for the most part, determine the magnitude of u. For want of somewhat better terms, those
factors may be characterized as (1) the flexibility of the capital stock,
and (2) the imperfect substitutability of labor for capital. Taking these
matters in turn we consider first the effect of the flexibility of the

---

[5] For a statement of the customary static formulation of the law of
diminishing returns see John M. Cassels, "On the Law of Variable
Proportions," in Readings in the Theory of Income Distribution.
Philadelphia: The Blakiston Co., 1946, pp. 103-118.

capital stock. It is obvious that, other things equal, the more flexible
the capital stock the less reduction of efficiency per man as a consequence of increases in the labor force. The degree of flexibility or
adaptability of the capital stock to changes in the proportions of the
other factors is determined by a number of conditions, the more important of which follow.[6]

(1) <u>Divisibility in the use of the capital stock</u>. Whether
capital goods are divisible or not is clearly important in determining
the extent to which increases in the labor force can be adapted to the
given capital stock. For example, some machines may be so specialized
that only a given number of workers can handle them and neither more
nor less. Such specialization can even exist for a given production
process. Many one-man machines are likely to be of this nature. Such
capital items as typewriters, linotype machines, electric drills, etc.
are items of this kind. Generally, it is likely that the more specialized
the machine the less flexible it is with respect to changes in the labor
force. This is especially likely to be the case where the machinery
sets the pace of the process and determines the rate of output per unit
of time. On the other hand, such capital items as office space or plant
space can often be adapted to accommodate a larger number of workers
without too much loss in efficiency per man. In a given production
process in which the raw materials go through a number of states before they come out as finished products the capital used in some stages
may be more divisible than that in others, but the least divisible capital
goods used in some necessary stage of production may determine the
degree to which more labor can be used in the process as a whole,
since there is little point in having more labor producing unfinished
goods that pile up at the least flexible "bottleneck" stage. In conclusion, it must be clear from such considerations as these that the more
divisible in use the capital stock is the less the magnitude of u as
population increases. If in a given productive process the capital is
not divisible at all then additional laborers added to the industry have

---

[6] Some of these factors have been considered, for the case of an individual firm, by George Stigler, "Production and Distribution in the
Short Run," <u>Journal of Political Economy</u>, Vol. 47, No. 3 (June, 1939),
pp. 305-327.

a marginal efficiency of zero. A developing economy with a growing population would be wise, other things being equal, to invest in capital that is as divisible in its use as is possible.

(2) Single-purpose vs. multi-purpose capital goods. By definition, it is clear that multi-purpose goods are more flexible than single-purpose goods. Certain capital goods may not be used to capacity in some processes. In such a case, when there are additions to the labor force, multi-purpose goods may conceivably be used for other and more productive processes rather than be more intensively or extensively employed in their original use, where their marginal efficiency may be lower.

(3) Expectation and planning in the construction of capital. The adaptability of a given type of capital to additions in the labor force depends clearly on the foresight of those who are instrumental in the construction of the capital. Those who plan and build capital goods may or may not take into account possible increases in labor force without proportional increases in capital goods. If foresight and adequate planning exist then it is conceivable that there could be built the kind of capital which would be most adaptable to expected changes in the proportions of the factors of production; whereas without foresight and adequate planning the capital stock is likely to be much less flexible than otherwise.

(4) The average length of life of the capital goods. Capital goods that depreciate very slowly and are replaced only after many years are likely to be very much less flexible than if the reverse is true. For it can readily be seen that the larger the proportion of the capital stock that is replaced each year, the larger the proportion that can be rebuilt in accordance with new conditions and new information, and the more readily adaptable the capital stock may become to increases in population. A rapidly developing country may not be acting in its best interests if it builds its capital of too durable a nature.

(5) Temporal substitutability of capital . In some cases an economy may be able to use the existing capital stock more intensively through such means as double shifts, etc. Although this results in the more rapid depreciation of the goods, it does lead to greater flexibility in two respects. First, through additional shifts a larger

labor force can be accommodated without too much loss in average productivity per man. Second, through shortening the average length of life of the capital goods, replacements for depreciated capital may be made more adaptable to new conditions.

(6) The demand structure for commodities. If in the industries in which capital is highly flexible, the demand for the goods produced is highly inelastic, and in the industries in which the capital is inflexible the demand is highly elastic with respect to national income, then the capital structure as a whole is effectively less flexible than if the reverse were true. Thus, the demand structure for commodities is indirectly, in part, a determinant of the magnitude of u.

The other major factors that determine the magnitude of u are the same as those that cause diminishing (or increasing) returns in the static theory of production. These matters have been considered in some detail in the existing economic literature and hence need not be taken up in detail here. Briefly stated, however, the major considerations are these. More labor means that each man has less capital, on the average, to work with. Thus, even if the capital stock were perfectly divisible, and there were no compensating advantages in the increased specialization of manpower with a greater labor force, we would expect a decrease in the productivity per man that was in some proportionate relation to the decrease in capital per man, and the previous ratio of capital to labor. But in addition to this there is the matter of the imperfect substitutability of labor for capital in the productive process. In view of this we would expect an additional decrease in the productivity per man as labor increased in those industries where the optimum proportion of labor to capital has been exceeded.[7]

---

[7] Even if capital were perfectly divisible there would still be an optimum ratio between capital and labor, beyond which additions in labor would cause a diminution in average output greater than that warranted by the decrease in capital per man. This is due to the fact that laborers are indivisible and cannot be made to fit smaller and smaller units of capital. For example, we would expect a more than proportionate loss in efficiency per man if twice as many truck drivers had to work with trucks that were half as small in every respect.

It must also be remembered that in a developing economy the structure of production is continually being changed through
innovations and investment in new industries. Such changes may conceivably lead to a somewhat lower magnitude of u than otherwise due
to one or more of several possibilities. (1) The new industries introduced into the economy may, at first, be subject to increasing returns with respect to increases in labor. (2) The new industries may
be somewhat less subject to diminishing returns than the existing ones
and hence the average overall loss due to decreases in labor is diminished. (3) Some new industries (or innovations) may make possible
such changes in the productive processes in other industries that
greater specialization of labor is both profitable and possible.

Varying Propensities to Invest

A, we may recall, is the proportion of the average income gain that is saved and invested during any period. It was assumed
above that this proportion was the same for all levels of g. But suppose
this is not the case. Suppose that at higher levels of the average income
gain a higher proportion is saved. This implies that higher levels of
average income result in a greater proportion of that average income
going into investment than do lower levels. In specific situations this
phenomenon may change the long run results of a given displacement
considerably. A is one of the components of the average income gain
multiplier (M). Although at lower levels of g, M may be less than
the maximum population multiplier (m), at higher levels of g, M
may be greater than m. Since M $>$ m is one of the necessary conditions for instability it follows that if M increases as g increases
then there is a better chance for a system to escape Malthusian equilibrium than otherwise.

Now it must be clear that A must have a maximum.
(For example, A cannot be greater than unity.) In those cases where
the maximum propensity to invest does not raise M above the rate
of the maximum population multiplier (m) the results are of the same
nature as they are for all the cases illustrated in Fig. 5, except case
III. On the other hand, if the maximum propensity to invest (A) can
raise M above the maximum m then there exists an initial positive
displacement of average income for which the system is unstable. It
is not necessary that the displacement be so large that initially M

be greater than m. In the early periods M may be less than the
population multiplier (m). All that is required is that the displacement be sufficiently large that the average income gain increases for
a certain number of periods. As g increases so does M, and if g
increases sufficiently a point will be reached at which M overtakes
m sufficiently for the system to be unstable.

In view of the foregoing argument the importance of
the size of the propensity to invest is obvious. The size of A may
determine whether attempts to raise average income and the standard
of living can or cannot be successful in the long run. Clearly, the
greater the size of A the greater the chances of success. An economy
may be able to raise the proportion of the national income which goes
into investment in a number of ways. One of the ways that immediately comes to mind is some kind of forced savings, either through increasing the quantity of bank credit, or though increasing government
indebtedness and direct government investment, or both. This is not
the place to consider the various possible means for an economy to
increase the magnitude of the propensity to save and invest. It is
sufficient to suggest that the value of A does not or need not depend
on the choices made by individual households and entrepreneurs alone.[8]

Changes in the Efficiency of Investment

In the original model the ratio between a unit of investment and the increment of average income created by that unit (if population had remained constant) was assumed to be constant. This ratio
between the increment of average income and investment was designated as B in our model. We consider in this section the question of
how this ratio is likely to change with respect to income changes, and
how such changing ratios affect the conclusions reached in Chapter IV.

First, however, it may be helpful to note the major

---

[8] An additional factor increasing the possibility of achieving instability via forced increases in A is the consideration that larger
savings and hence less average consumption may induce lower rates
of population growth than otherwise. Less average consumption may
cause higher mortality rates, later marriages, and perhaps lower
birth rates than otherwise. On this point see H. Bowen, "Capital in
Relation to Optimum Population," Social Forces, Vol. 15, No. 3
(March, 1937), pp. 346-350. See also J. J. Spengler, "Pareto on Population, I", Quarterly Journal of Economics, Vol. 58, No. 4 (Aug.,
1944), pp. 571-601.

factors that determine B. Essentially, they are the factors that determine the nature and productivity of the additions to capital stock
which are made period by period. These factors are briefly as follows:

      (1) The nature of the investment alternatives
available.

      (2) The extent of knowledge about investment alterna-
tives.

      (3) The availability of skilled individuals of various
types in the managerial, entrepreneurial, and labor categories.

      (4) The scientific and cultural equipment available in
the economy and the availability of means for turning out skilled individuals.

      (5) The mobility of the labor force.

      (6) The availability of markets and the terms of trade
between goods produced in this economy and elsewhere.

      (7) The extent to which government activities deter-
mine the nature of investment through tariffs, trade restrictions,
taxes, subsidies, and through direct investment.

      Factors (1) and (2) determine the opportunities for
investment that are known to individuals instrumental in making investment decisions. Some kinds of investment require the existence
of special skills that may not be available in an underdeveloped
country, hence factors (3) and (4). Economic development usually
requires a shift in the labor force from some areas and industries to
others, and a highly immobile labor force may preclude the possibility or advisability of certain types of investment. Factor (6) is
self-explanatory. Finally, the role and nature of the government must
be taken into account.

      The question that arises is how the ratio changes as
additional units of investment are added. Is this ratio an increasing
function of average income, a decreasing one, some combination of
both, or some function that is not easily describable in a few words?
This question cannot be answered in any definite way on an a priori
basis since there are various conceivable factors that lead to different results depending on the relative magnitudes of the component
factors. The problem is further complicated by the fact that the
ratio (B) depends on many factors other than income. However,

abstracting from significant economic inventions, a reasonable case
can be made for assuming that B is either (1) first an increasing
and then a decreasing function of average income, or (2) a decreasing
function of average income from the outset. The first assumption implies that in the early stages of economic development additional units
of capital would yield increasing increments to average income if population remained constant, while in the later stages of development
this trend would be reversed. The second assumption implies that
from the outset additional units of capital would yield diminishing increments to average income even if population remained constant.

There are two significant factors that may lead to increasing values of B. These are external economies and specialization. External economies are likely to be most significant in the
earlier stages of industrialization. That is, such things as transportation systems, sources of power, etc., usually require a very large
fixed capital at the outset and as a result become more efficiently
utilized as industrial growth takes place. Beyond some point the in-
creasingly efficient use of fixed assets disappears as the fixed capital
approaches capacity utilization. This analysis follows along the usual
classical and neo-classical lines, and is essentially the same sort of
argument that has been so ably stated by the late Prof. Allyn Young
in his article "Increasing Returns and Economic Progress."[9] In brief,
it all goes back to Adam Smith's famous dictum about the division of
labor being limited by the extent of the market. The greater the extent
of the market the greater the division of labor. But the extent of the market is essentially determined by the level of income. Increasing the level
of income leads to a larger market which in turn permits greater specialization, industrial differentiation, and more roundabout methods of production. Greater industrial differentiation and specialization lead, in
part, to external economies which in turn reduce costs and increase income. There are of course limits to industrial differentiation and specialization due in part to the increasing cost of coordination of factors
and in part to the relative fixity of certain factors of production.

---

[9] Economic Journal, Vol. 38, No. 152 (Dec., 1928), pp. 527-542. See
also George J. Stigler, "The Division of Labor is Limited by the Extent
of the Market," The Journal of Political Economy, Vol. 59, No. 3 (June,
1951), pp. 185-193.

On the other side of the picture, if the additional units of investment consist of the same types as the previous units then diminishing returns to scale set in at some point. If the successive investment units are of a different composition than the previous ones then presumably the highest yielding investment units are chosen first and the lower yielding investment units are chosen later. In any event, beyond some point we would get declining values of B.

Some of the empirical evidence related to this question may be of interest. E. H. Stern in investigating the relationship between net capital expenditures and net national income for the United Kingdom, U. S. A., Germany and South Africa came to the conclusion that the more economically developed the country, the greater the additions to capital required to obtain a unit increase in output. Stern finds, for example, that it takes 3.3 units of new capital in the United Kingdom or the U. S. A. to get a unit increase in output, while 2.5 units of capital will yield a unit increase in output in South Africa.[10] Of course these empirical ratios are not quite the same as our B since, among other things, they do not exclude the effects of population growth. Although this evidence cannot be considered as a confirmation of any sort, it is comforting that these empirical instances do not contradict our hypotheses.

The above considerations do not take into account exceptional inventions and innovations which may come at any point in the course of development, and which may at such a point change the value of B considerably. All that can be said with respect to such inventions is that they cannot be accounted for in the general theory and hence it is probably best to consider their effects as exogenous displacements.

Let us now consider the effects of these assumptions on our model. It will be recalled that both B and A are components of M. Thus if both B and A increase as average income increases then M increases in the same manner. Now, it has been argued in the previous section that A must have a maximum. Also, beyond some level of average income B decreases and hence works in the

---

[10] "Capital Requirements in Progressive Economies," *Economica*, New Series, Vol. 12, No. 47 (Aug., 1945), pp. 163-171.

opposite direction of A. Hence it follows that B must have some maximum and therefore M must have some maximum value. This holds
also for the case where B is throughout a decreasing function of y.
Hence introducing our new assumptions about the nature of B does not
change the general shape of the relationship between M and average
income that was assumed in the previous section, although the exact
magnitudes would differ. We thus conclude that up to some point M is
an increasing function of average income and beyond some point a decreasing function. Since the effect of this assumption was already analyzed in the previous section we need not go into it again.

Changes in Income Distribution

In the above discussion we assumed that the income distribution remains constant throughout. But clearly this need not be the
case. As average income rises the income distribution may become
skewed toward the upper income groups. That is, as g increases we
may have a lesser proportion of the population in the middle income
groups, a somewhat greater proportion of the population in the lower
income groups, and more than proportionately higher absolute incomes
for those remaining in the higher income groups. On the basis (and
general observation) that people with higher incomes save a larger proportion of their incomes than those with lower incomes, the effect of
such a phenomenon is a propensity to save and invest of greater magnitude than otherwise. Of course, an income distribution that is skewed
toward the lower end of the income range as average income increases
has a depressing effect on the propensity to save. The consequence of
changing values of A has already been considered above.

Changes in income distribution may, at the same time
that they affect A, also affect the rate of population growth. It may be
argued that an income distribution which is skewed toward the upper
income ranges as g increases has a somewhat depressing effect on
population growth since the reduced share of the national income that
goes to the more numerous lower income groups increases death rates
and decreases birth rates. On the basis of similar reasoning, an income distribution that is skewed toward the lower end of the income
range results in a greater rate of population growth than otherwise.
Thus, changing income distributions that favor higher income groups
as a g increases result in higher M's and lower m's than otherwise,

while the reverse is true for changing income distributions that favor lower income groups as g increases.

Changing Age Distributions as Population Increases

We have assumed thus far that the age distribution of the population remains constant as population increases. This assumption is contrary to whatever historical evidence appears to exist on the matter.[11] What happens to the age distribution as average income and population increase depends on the changes in fertility and age-specific mortality that take place. The usual experience is for death rates to decline most in the youngest age groups as average income increases. The initial effect of such a change is for the ratio of young people to older people to increase. Thus the ratio of those in the labor force to those not in the labor force diminishes.

A decrease in the labor force to total population depresses average income -- other things being equal. The effect on average income is similar to the effect of an additional increase in population when the labor force to total population ratio remains constant. Thus, the effect on average income is really the same as that of a slight increase in r. It is clear at once that such decreases in average income due to an adverse change in the labor force-total population ratio constitutes an additional hurdle in any attempt to achieve the instability of the system. A given positive displacement has less chance of overcoming the average income depressing forces because of this initial change in the age distribution.

However, should the increases in average income (and g) continue and some declines in fertility set in then sooner or later the new birth cohorts entering the population will be smaller than the previous birth cohorts and, as a consequence, the ratio of those in the working ages to those in the total population will increase. The effect of this will be to increase the ratio of labor force to population size, to decrease the economic burden of dependency, and hence to increase average real income. Thus, beyond a value of g, the changing age distribution is likely to make it easier for a given displacement to result in an escape from Malthusian conditions. In conclusion, it would

---

[11] Cf. United Nations, World Population Trends, 1920-1947. Lake Success, 1949, pp. 15 ff. Also, United Kingdom, Royal Commission on Population, Report. London: His Majesty's Stationery Office, 1949, pp. 88 ff.

appear that as g increases from its initial magnitude the changing
age distribution shifts from an average income depressing force to an
average income elevating one, if fertility begins to decline at some
point.

APPENDIX TO CHAPTER VI

NUMERICAL EXAMPLES

The numerical examples worked out and presented be-
low follow the system of equations outlined in Chapter IV, but the population growth function has the same general shape as that postulated
in Chapter VI. The population growth function is presented in Table
I. It can be seen from the table that up to a point it is monotonic increasing, and beyond that point it is monotonic decreasing with respect
to the average income gain.

At the outset the system is assumed to be in equilibrium.
The following additional assumptions are made: In each of the three
examples the beginning population size (P_1) is assumed to be 100
(say, 100 million). (Line 1, column 5.) The value of u is in each
case assumed to be 1. That is, an increase in population size by one
unit depresses average income by one unit. In Example I (also curve
I, Fig. 8) the initial positive displacement from average income is
200 units (see Table II, line 1, column 8). In Example II, the initial
displacement is 215 units, and in Example III the displacement is 225
units.

The basic equation employed in computation was

$$g_t = M g_{t-1} - r_{t-1} P_{t-1} u.$$

The computations (see Table II) were made as follows:

Column 1. The figures in this column indicate the period
numbers (i.e. the value of t).

Column 2. The figures in this column indicate the population size at the beginning of the period. This figure is the same as
the population size at the end of the previous period, and is obtained
by copying the figure in column 5 in the line above.

97

Column 3. The figures in this column indicate the rates of population growth appropriate for the period. The value of g is shown in column 6. The appropriate rates for each period are obtained by noting the value of g_{t-1} and referring to Table I.

Column 4. The figures in this column are obtained by multiplying column 2 by column 3, which yields the absolute amount of population increase, and then multiplying by the value of u which is unity.

Column 5. Equals column 2 plus column 4. Since u is equal to one, column 4 also shows the amount of population growth.

Column 6. The value of g for the previous period. Hence, these figures are the same as those on the line above in column 8.

Column 7. Column 6 X 1.02. The value of M is assumed to be 1.02.

Column 8. Column 7 minus column 4.

Column 9. This column indicates the changes in the value of g from period to period.

All the examples are computed in exactly the same manner, except that the beginning displacements are different.

The results of the three examples are shown in Fig. 8. The ordinates represent the figures in column 8, the abscissas the figures in column 1. In the computations that were made each year was computed separately, but for illustrative purposes it is sufficient to show the figures for approximately every fifth year. These are shown in Table II.

TABLE I

THE POPULATION GROWTH FUNCTION

Rate of Growth r_{t-1} (per cent)	g_{t-1}
1.1	200 plus*
1.2	205 "
1.3	210 "
1.4	215 "
1.5	220 "
1.6	225 "
1.7	230 "
1.8	235 "
1.9	240 "
2.0	245 "
2.1	255 "
2.2	265 "
2.3	275 "
2.2	285 "
2.1	295 "
2.0	305 "
1.9	315 "
1.8	325 "
1.7	335 "
1.6	345 "
1.5	355 "
1.4	365 "
1.3	375 "
1.2	385 "
1.1	395 "
1.0	405 "
.9	415 "
.8	425 "
.7	435 "

* The rate of growth of 1.1% in the left-hand column applies to all values of g of 200 and above, but below 205. Similarly, all other rates of growth are applicable in the same manner.

       MODIFICATIONS OF THE DYNAMIC MODEL

TABLE II

EXAMPLE I:

Computation of the Magnitudes of g Over Time for an Initial Displacement of 200 and $M = 1.02$

(1)	(2)	(3)	(4)	(5)	(6)	(7)	(8)	(9)
	Population Size at Beginning of Period	Rate of Population Growth During Period		Population Size at End of Period		Col. (6) X 1.02	Average Income Above Equilibrium	First Differences
Period Number								
t	P_{t-1}	r_{t-1}	$P_{t-1}r_{t-1}u$	P_t	g_{t-1}	Mg_{t-1}	g_t	g_t-g_{t-1}
1				100.			200.	
2	100.00	1.1	1.10	101.10	200.	204.00	202.90	
3	101.10	1.1	1.11	102.21	202.90	206.96	205.85	2.90
4	102.21	1.2	1.23	103.44	205.85	209.97	208.74	2.95
								2.89
10	110.55	1.5	1.66	112.21	223.08	227.54	225.88	2.80
15	119.80	1.8	2.16	121.96	236.69	241.42	239.26	2.57
20	131.50	2.0	2.63	134.13	249.18	254.16	251.53	2.35
25	145.47	2.1	3.05	148.52	260.59	265.80	262.75	2.16
30	161.71	2.2	3.56	165.27	270.84	276.26	272.70	1.86
35	180.66	2.3	4.16	184.82	279.34	284.93	280.77	1.43
40	202.42	2.2	4.45	206.87	285.79	291.51	287.06	1.27
45	225.68	2.2	4.96	230.64	291.36	297.19	292.23	.87
50	251.62	2.2	5.54	257.16	294.70	300.59	295.05	.35
55	279.45	2.1	5.87	285.32	296.41	302.34	296.47	.06
60	301.06	2.1	6.51	306.57	295.43	301.34	294.83	- .60
65	345.35	2.2	7.60	352.95	289.50	295.29	287.69	-1.81
70	385.80	2.3	8.87	394.67	277.58	283.13	274.26	-3.32
75	430.14	2.1	9.03	439.17	260.33	265.54	256.51	-3.82
79	466.51	1.9	8.86	475.37	244.32	249.21	240.35	-3.97

TABLE II (Continued)

EXAMPLE II:

Computation of the Magnitudes of g Over Time for an Initial Displacement of 215 and $M = 1.02$

(1)	(2)	(3)	(4)	(5)	(6)	(7)	(8)	(9)
	Population Size at Beginning of Period	Rate of Population Growth During Period		Population Size at End of Period		Col. (6) X 1.02	Average Income Above Equilibrium	First Differences
Period Number								
t	P_{t-1}	r_{t-1}	$P_{t-1}r_{t-1}u$	P_t	g_{t-1}	Mg_{t-1}	g_t	g_t-g_{t-1}
1				100.			215.	
2	100.	1.4	1.40	101.40	215.	219.30	217.90	
3	101.40	1.4	1.42	102.82	217.90	222.26	220.84	2.90
4	102.82	1.5	1.54	104.36	220.84	225.26	223.72	2.94
								2.88
10	113.20	1.8	2.04	115.24	237.82	242.58	240.54	2.72
15	124.49	2.0	2.49	126.98	250.85	255.87	253.38	2.53
20	137.86	2.1	2.90	140.76	263.07	268.33	265.43	2.36
25	153.56	2.2	3.38	156.94	274.15	279.63	276.25	2.10
30	171.88	2.3	3.95	175.83	283.64	289.31	285.36	1.72
35	191.82	2.2	4.22	196.04	292.41	298.26	294.04	1.63
40	213.25	2.1	4.48	217.73	300.55	306.56	302.08	1.53
45	236.37	2.0	4.73	241.10	307.78	313.94	309.21	1.43
50	260.98	2.0	5.22	266.20	314.22	320.50	315.28	1.06
55	287.01	1.9	5.45	292.46	319.84	326.24	320.79	.95
60	315.33	1.9	5.99	321.32	323.68	330.15	324.16	.48
65	346.45	1.8	6.24	352.69	325.00	331.50	325.26	.26
70	378.78	1.8	6.82	385.60	325.21	331.71	324.89	- .32
75	415.76	1.9	7.90	423.66	320.61	327.02	319.12	-1.49
79	448.27	2.0	8.97	457.24	313.55	319.82	310.85	-2.70

TABLE II (Continued)

EXAMPLE III:

Computation of the Magnitudes of g Over Time for an Initial Displacement of 225 and $M = 1.02$

(1)	(2)	(3)	(4)	(5)	(6)	(7)	(8)	(9)
Period Number	Population Size at Beginning of Period	Rate of Population Growth During Period		Population Size at End of Period		Col. (6) X 1.02	Average Income Above Equilibrium	First Differences
t	P_{t-1}	r_{t-1}	$P_{t-1}r_{t-1}u$	P_t	g_{t-1}	Mg_{t-1}	g_t	$g_t - g_{t-1}$
1				100.			225.	
2	100.	1.6	1.60	101.60	225.	229.50	227.90	2.90
3	101.60	1.6	1.63	103.23	227.90	232.46	230.83	2.93
4	103.23	1.7	1.75	104.98	230.83	235.45	233.70	2.87
10	114.88	2.0	2.30	117.18	247.73	252.68	250.38	2.65
15	127.08	2.1	2.67	129.75	260.83	266.05	263.38	2.55
20	141.40	2.2	3.11	144.51	273.10	278.56	275.45	2.35
25	158.26	2.3	3.64	161.90	283.99	289.67	286.03	2.04
30	176.62	2.2	3.89	180.51	294.45	300.34	296.45	2.00
35	196.15	2.1	4.12	200.27	304.78	310.88	306.76	1.98
40	216.79	1.9	4.12	220.91	315.04	321.34	317.22	2.18
45	238.19	1.8	4.29	242.48	325.57	332.08	327.79	2.22
50	260.40	1.7	4.43	264.83	336.36	343.09	338.66	2.30
55	283.03	1.6	4.53	287.56	347.82	354.78	350.25	2.43
60	305.80	1.5	4.59	310.39	360.32	367.52	362.93	2.61
65	328.47	1.4	4.60	333.07	374.22	381.70	377.10	2.88
70	350.38	1.2	4.20	354.58	390.35	398.16	393.96	3.61
75	370.44	1.0	3.70	374.14	410.07	418.27	414.57	4.50
79	384.71	0.8	3.08	387.79	429.15	437.73	434.65	5.50

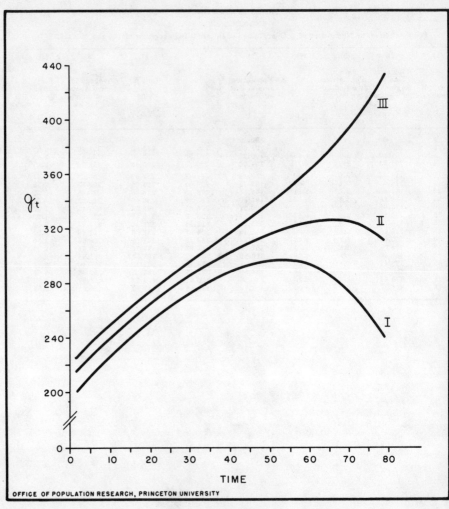

FIGURE 8

CHAPTER VII

SOME ELEMENTS OF A MULTI-SECTOR MODEL

Introduction

The models discussed in the previous chapters are in
the form and spirit of macro-economics. An objection may be raised
that such models, which are only in terms of aggregates and derivations of aggregates such as averages, omit or fail to reveal significant
interactions between entities which constitute the aggregates.. There
is some validity to this argument. First, the aggregative approach may
conceivably give a false picture of what occurs, for it may happen
that the entities constituting the heterogeneous aggregates are so related, or behave in such a manner, as to reveal different processes
of demographic-economic development than those revealed by working
with aggregates alone. Second, it is conceivable that for some purposes one may want to put greater weight on the progress of some
sectors of the economy than on others; and, of course, an aggregative
model would not reveal the relative progress made by different sectors. Third, the relationships between sectors may, in part, determine the magnitudes of the central variables for the economy as a
whole. Hence, to understand the determination of the aggregates it
may be necessary to examine the relations between different sectors.
Last, but by no means least, working with aggregates may hide or ob-
scure factors, interdependencies or relationships that may turn out to
be of great heuristic value.

For the reasons just indicated an attempt is made in
this chapter (1) to discuss the central economic and demographic
interdependencies and activities which can occur between various sectors of an economy, (2) to delineate those inter-sector relations which
are in conformity with the models considered previously and those

103

which are not, and (3) to illustrate by an example the type of inter-
sector models which can be constructed.

The Notion of a Sector

By a sector we shall mean any subdivision of the total
population in which membership within a subdivision is defined in such
a way that any person belongs to one and only one subdivision. Some
of the more obvious possible bases for subdivision that come to mind
are (a) by industry, (b) by occupational groupings, (c) by income groupings, (d) by geographical area, (e) by religious or racial groupings,
and so on. Subdivisions may, of course, be made by more than one
type of classification; for example, the subdivisions may be made both
by industry and by age groupings. On an a priori basis very little can
be said about the type of subdivision that is best. Generally speaking
we would expect that schemes of subdivision that yield sectors which
are microcosms of the whole will add little to our knowledge, while
subdivision into sectors more homogeneous than the whole is likely to
yield more information than the aggregative analysis.

One of the first questions to consider is the basis upon
which the division of the population is to be made. Several criteria
come to mind. First, the scheme of subdivision should be so chosen
that the possible relationships between the sectors should be of a kind
that tell us something interesting about the processes of demographic-
economic development. Further, the revealed relationships should be
such that we get more insight into or information about these processes
than we would obtain by using less complicated, more aggregative models.
For there is no point in worrying about inter-sector relationships if
they add nothing to our knowledge. Second, the subdivision should be
such as to increase the probability of obtaining more reliable be-
havior-equations for the sectors than could be obtained by considering
only the aggregate. It is conceivable that suitably chosen sectors may
permit the determination of behavior patterns which are reasonably
constant over time whereas the heterogeneous aggregates may not permit such determinations. Where this is not the case then, other things
being equal, we would be worse off working with a multi-sector model
that with an aggregative model. Third, it is desirable that the subdivision be such as to better reveal latent demographic and economic
characteristics than would be revealed by an aggregative analysis.

For example, a functional relationship between, say, population growth and other variables for the aggregative model may not lead to as reliable an assessment of future trends (or latent developments), once the parameters of the function are statistically determined, as we would get by working with a set of such relationships for suitably chosen more homogeneous sectors. Of course, this last need not be the case, but it is a possibility to be taken into account. And fourth, where there is an intrinsic interest in studying the changes that take place for some sectors of the population as against others, then of course the contemplated subdivision should permit the study of such changes.

In the previous chapters it was either implicitly or explicitly assumed that average income was the index of progress. However, given other criteria of progress or development it is conceivable that increases in average income may not be concomitant with economic improvement. This is especially likely to be the case if greater stress or value is placed on the improvement of some sectors of the economy than on others. Thus it is possible for those in one sector not to improve their economic position at all, and the average for the aggregate to increase. If one judges improvement by the position of that particular group whose position did not improve then the result for the aggregate is misleading. In such a case a sector analysis is indispensable.

In this connection the question arises whether improvement within a sector is best attained by direct investment within that sector, or by some other method of aid to the sector, or whether in the long run improvement is most readily achieved indirectly via investment to other sectors. This, of course, will depend on the extent and nature of the interrelationships that go on between sectors. In order to answer questions of this kind an attempt will be made later to expand one of the basic equations of the earlier models so that inter-sector relationships are connected with the aggregative system.

An Outline of Major Inter-Sector Relationships

Where there are no inter-sector relationships the analysis of a multi-sector model is trivial, for in such a case the net outcome for the economy as a whole is the simple aggregation of the outcomes of each of the sectors. Without inter-sector relationships we would simply treat each sector as a separate economic unit and add the results. The type of analysis for each sector would be the same

as that outlined in the previous chapters. In such a case no new problems are involved. Thus, the new interesting elements in a multi-
sector model are the inter-sector relationships.

There are two broad categories of activities we shall
be concerned with: those connected with the distribution of investment
between sectors and those connected with shifts in population between
sectors. Of course, it is recognized that investment shifts and population shifts are related to each other. Indeed, the purpose of the next
section is to delineate the connection between such movements. For
the present, however, it may be useful to note the major activities we
have in mind when we speak rather loosely about inter-sector relationships. The reader will note that these activities are similar to those
considered by students of international trade, with the exception that
(a) we are not concerned with currency problems, and (b) that we are
very much concerned with labor shifts whereas in international trade
theory it is usually assumed that inter-country labor movements are
either absent or unimportant.

(1) Inter-sector trade affecting price and income
changes. Trade between the members of different sectors will influence the prices paid for commodities consumed by members of different sectors and for the prices paid to productive agents. These
prices will in part influence the total and average incomes enjoyed by
members of the various sectors. To illustrate these points consider
for a moment a two sector economy, calling the sectors I and II, in
which there is an exogenous injection of capital in sector I but not in
II. The immediate effect of this event is that sector I, which now
possesses more capital resources than before, will now be able to produce more units of whatever it is producing. The prices of the goods
produced in sector I are now likely to decline, while the prices of those
goods purchased by the members of sector I but not produced within
that sector are likely to rise. The extent of the price changes will be
to a considerable degree determined by the nature of the demand functions of the goods produced in the two sectors. Other things equal,
average income in sector I will rise but not to the extent of the increase in its productive power. Since the terms of trade have gone in
favor of sector II average income in sector II will also increase to
some extent. Thus the price changes induce income changes that would

not occur otherwise. Of course, this is not the net upshot of the matter since other inter-sector relationships are at work simultaneously.

(2) Inter-sector price-income effects causing changes in investment. The price and income changes discussed above will induce changes in the magnitude and distribution of investment. Continuing with our two sector example we can trace other likely (but by no means necessary) effects. The increase in incomes in both sectors is likely to induce greater savings and investment. The relative price changes will determine in part the relative profitability of various lines of endeavor and will hence determine, again in part, the distribution of the factors between sectors. Of course, the supply functions of the various factors of production must be taken into account.

(3) Complementarities in production and consumption causing investment changes. Investment in one sector will be determined by changes in the production and consumption activities going on in the other sectors. For example, if a new industry is started in sector I then it may be profitable for the members of sector II to invest in a complementary industry, or in an industry that provides raw materials and services for the new industry. Similarly the introduction of a new consumers good induces the introduction or increased production of complementary consumer goods. Also, the increase in the output of an existing good will set in motion increases in complementary activities in various sectors of the economy.

(4) Labor force shifts. This category of inter-sector activities is almost self explanatory. Shifts in labor force may be induced by a variety of causes. Wage changes, differential investment rates and changes in the labor supply within sectors due to differing rates of population growth are all possible causes of labor force reallocations. The reallocation of the labor force between sectors has, in turn, significant economic effects. The first and most obvious is that the reallocation of labor changes the marginal and total productivity of both labor and capital. If the nature and motives of the labor force shifts follow along the lines of economic rationality then the redistribution of the labor force increases total and average real incomes. Following the neo-classical analysis we would expect labor to shift from those sectors where its marginal productivity is low to those where it is relatively high. Also we would expect the shifts to go from

sectors where labor meets with diminishing returns to sectors where
increasing returns are possible -- should such sectors exist. The
shifts that take place also benefit those remaining in sectors where a
net outflow of population has taken place since the marginal productivit
of those remaining increases as the number of laborers in diminishing
returns sectors declines. It is important to note that for any labor
shift to or from a sector to be economically rational it is not necessar;
that a visible improvement or increase in average income take place.
The labor force shifts may be rational even though average incomes
decline in some sectors or decline universally. All that is necessary
for the labor force redistribution to be economically rational is that
the position in each sector after the shifts be better than it would be
had the shifts never taken place. Thus the visible aftermath of a shift
in labor between sectors might be a decline in average income, but the
decline would have been greater for other reasons had the labor shifts
never taken place.

Population shifts, in addition to implying a redistributio:
of the labor force between sectors, also change the location of consumers, alter the distribution of skills between sectors, and influence
the relative attractiveness of investment outlets. A change in the distribution of consumers and of economic skills will of itself change the
relative attractiveness of investment outlets. But in addition the labor
force redistribution alters the marginal efficiencies of capital between
sectors, and as a consequence alters the attractiveness of investment
between sectors.

(5) Demographic changes caused by inter-sector economic changes. To the extent that inter-sector economic activities
affect average income they will affect mortality rates and probably
fertility rates, which in turn will alter the size and distribution of the
labor force. Also, inter-sector economic activities may change the
nature and proportion of the occupational duties carried out within a
sector which again are likely to affect morbidity and mortality rates.
Since the health and longevity of potential parents are related to the
probability of having offspring, changes in mortality rates will indirectly affect fertility rates. Also, it is conceivable that occupational
changes may affect mores and practices relating to marriage, mating,
birth control, and so on, so that the occupational changes have a direct

effect on fertility. The list of possible demographic changes as a consequence of inter-sector economic changes, as well as the chain of
causation, can be expanded readily but enough has been said to indicate
the type of phenomena we have in mind.

(6) Inter-sector services that affect mortality within a
sector. An increase and change in the economic activities in sector I
may make available services and goods to sector II that directly decrease mortality in the latter sector. For example the training in one
sector of physicians and nurses whose services are made available to
other sectors is likely to affect mortality (and also fertility) in these
other sectors. Similarly other goods and services which aid health
and welfare that are produced in one sector may benefit other sectors
through their becoming generally available. Economic gains in one
sector may make it possible, either through taxation or other means,
to increase the public health activities for the community as a whole,
to the benefit of other sectors.

(7) Inter-sector flow of information, mores, habits,
etc. that affects fertility and mortality. This category represents the
most amorphous type of inter-sector effects -- a type that is difficult
to pin down and yet cannot be completely ignored. There can be no
question but that mores, habits, values, and recognized ways of doing
things (cultural patterns) do have some effects on fertility and mortality. To the extent that such mores, values, and cultural patterns can
be influenced by events in their sectors, these influences will alter the
mores and cultural patterns within a sector which in turn will affect
fertility, mortality and migration. One way in which such transfers
take place is through the spread of new ideas and information between
sectors, that is, via the vehicles of inter-sector and intra-sector communication which may exist. Thus, a change in outlook and mores in
one sector, due to an intra-sector event(s), may spread to other sectors
and affect fertility, marriage, and mortality rates in the other sectors.
An exact analysis of such events is of course extremely difficult. One
source of difficulty lies in the fact that such concepts as general outlook, mores, and values are vague and indistinct. In view of this an
attempt will be made in the next chapter to give greater precision to
concepts of this type, as well as to indicate the relationship of such
concepts to the general models we have been trying to build. But this

subject is so complex and can lead us down so many byways that only some of the elementary aspects of the problem will be considered.

The Basic Identity for a Multi-Sector Model

Thus far we have merely attempted to categorize and discuss very briefly the inter-sectional economic and demographic relationships which may influence the course of demographic-economic development. Now, we can see something of the way in which these relationships are connected to our models discussed in earlier chapters by expanding one of our earlier equations.

For the economy as a whole the equation that relates activities in one time period with the change in average income in the next is as follows:[1]

$$\Delta g_{t+1} = A_t B_t g_t - r_t u_t P_t \quad \text{or,} \tag{1}$$

$$\Delta y_{t+1} = A_t B_t g_t - r_t u_t P_t \tag{1a}$$

where g_t is the difference between actual average income and equilibrium average income, A_t is the proportion of g_t that goes into investment, B_t is the ratio between the amount of average investment and the average income resulting in the next period due to this average investment if population size remains constant, r_t is the rate of population increase between period t and the succeeding period, u_t is the amount of decrease in average income per unit of population

---

[1] Δy_{t+1} stands for the increase in average income between period t and period t+1. Δy_{t+1} is of course the same as the increase in g_{t+1} between the two periods. As long as $A_t B_t g_t$ is greater than $r_t u_t P_t$ then the average income is increasing. The symbols employed in this section are the same as those used in the previous two chapters.

increase, and P_t is the population size. All subscripts refer to time periods. (This equation is similar to one that is employed in Chapter IV.)

It is important to note that equation (1) can be interpreted in such a way that it is an identity. An identity is, of course, not a conceivably falsifiable proposition but it may nevertheless be very useful in giving insight into the operation of the system.[2] Equation (1) is an identity if we interpret the magnitudes of A_t, B_t, r_t, and u_t, as ex post rather than ex ante. That is, A_t, B_t, r_t, and u_t, will take on certain values in period t so as to yield the actual outcome for period t+1. In other words, after the event we could calculate the values of A_t and r_t which did occur and we know that there are values for B_t and u_t (which we may or may not be able to estimate in practice) that will give us the correct outcome for Δg_{t+1}. (As usual we have in mind only a closed economy.) If we restrict the magnitudes of the four variables in some way, or if we assume that certain functional relationships hold between some of the variables and the parameters then, of course, we no longer have an identity but a theory of the determination of Δg_t (and hence average income) over time; i.e., a theory of how average income changes over time.

Before continuing with the derivation of the identity there is a second point that is worthy of note. In equation (1) we assume that there is some value of average income that is the Malthusian equilibrium value, and g_t is calculated on the basis of this value. Now, we can substitute average income (y_t) for g_t and obtain a similar identity on the basis of average income rather than the average income gain (g_t). If we do this A_t has to be interpreted as the proportion of average income that goes into average investment. For empirical work it is conceivable that the identity in terms of average income rather than in terms of g_t may be more useful since it might very well be impossible to estimate what the Malthusian equilibrium average income is. In what follows it is important to note that, keeping in mind the different interpretations of A_t we can readily

---

[2] Examples from economics of identities that are useful in giving insight into the operation of a system are the Fisher and Cambridge equations used in monetary theory.

switch from one identity to the other without difficulty.

Now let us consider what our identity would look like for a single sector. We assume that there are s sectors, running from 1, 2, ..., s. We now add second subscripts to our variables and parameters to denote different sectors. Let the subscript j denote the typical sector. If no inter-sector events take place then the identity for sector j is as follows:

$$\Delta g_{t+1,j} = A_{tj} B_{tj} g_{tj} - r_{tj} u_{tj} P_{tj} \qquad (2)$$

Since our purpose is to account for inter-sector events equation (2) has to be enlarged so that it includes capital movements and population movements between sectors. The amount saved in sector j during period t is $A_{tj}g_{tj}$. However, the members of sector j need not invest all of their savings within the sector. Some savings will be invested in sectors other than those in which they originate. Let $a_{tj}g_{tj}$ denote the difference between per capita investment coming from other sectors into sector j and the amount of per capita investment made by members of sector j in other sectors. It is important to note that the per capita calculations always refer to the same sector. Thus, $a_{tj}g_{tj}$ is equal to total investment entering sector j minus total investment leaving sector j divided by the population in sector j. Also, a_{tj} is some proportion of g_{tj} that is either positive or negative, depending on whether "net average investment imports" $(a_{tj}g_{tj})$ are positive or negative. It follows from the above that average investment in sector j is represented by $(A_{tj} + a_{tj})g_{tj}$.

In order to include inter-sectional population shifts in our equation let $R_{tj}P_{tj}$ denote the net population movements in and out of sector j. That is to say, $R_{tj}P_{tj}$ is the difference between the number of people who enter sector j from other sectors and the number who leave sector j for other sectors. R_{tj} is of course some proportion of P_{tj} which is either positive or negative. Given this, the net population change that takes place within sector j can be written $(r_{tj} + R_{tj})P_{tj}$.

We are now in a position to rewrite equation (2) to include the inter-sectional investment and population shifts that take place simultaneously. We therefore have equation (3) as the identity for the typical sector, sector j.[3]

(3) $\Delta g_{tj} = (A_{tj} + a_{tj}) B_{tj} g_{tj} - (r_{tj} + R_{tj}) P_{tj} u_{tj}$

Now, it is useful to aggregate the right hand sides of equations (2) and (3) so that we can develop algebraic expressions which permit us to compare the operation of the system without inter-sector activities with the operation of the system where there are inter-sector activities.

The relationship between the increase in the average income gain for the economy as a whole (Δg_t) and the sum of the increases in the average income gains for each of the sectors follows readily from the averaging process. This relationship is

(4) $$\Delta g_t = \frac{\sum_{j=1}^{s} \Delta g_{tj} P_{tj}}{P_t} \quad \text{or,} \quad \Delta g_{t+1} = \frac{\sum_j \Delta g_{t+1,j} P_{t+1,j}}{P_{t+1}}$$

where the equilibrium average income for each sector is the same. However, where the equilibrium average income is not the same for each sector equation (4) has a sensible and somewhat more general interpretation. In this case Δg_t is the increase in the average income gain with the understanding that for each sector the average income gain is calculated on the basis of its own equilibrium average income.[4] This latter formulation is both more general and more reasonable since it is likely that the equilibrium average income for the various sectors will not be alike.

Using similar symbols to those employed in Chapter IV the relationship between the population size of sector j in one period and the next is given by

---

[3] For a closed economy $\sum_{j=1}^{s} a_{tj} g_{tj} = 0$, and $\sum_{j=1}^{s} R_{tj} P_{tj} = 0$.

[4] In reading the equations that follow it may help to keep in mind that Δg_{t+1} is always equal to Δy_{t+1}. Hence we could interpret Δg_{t+1} as the increase in average income.

$$P_{tj} = m_{tj}P_{tj} \qquad (5)$$

Aggregating the right hand side of equation (2) for all sectors and averaging we obtain

$$\Delta g_{t+1} = \frac{\sum\limits_{j=1}^{s} A_{tj}B_{tj}g_{tj}m_{tj}P_{tj} - \sum\limits_{j=1}^{s} r_{tj}P_{tj}u_{tj}m_{tj}P_{tj}}{P_{t+1}} \qquad (6)$$

The right hand side of equation (6) without the summation signs indicates the contribution that sector j makes to the change in average income for the economy as a whole. For ease in exposition it is best not to worry about the denominator of the right hand side of equation (6). We therefore rewrite (6)

$$\Delta g_{t+1}P_{t+1} = \sum\limits_{j=1}^{s} A_{tj}B_{tj}g_{tj}m_{tj}P_{tj} - \sum\limits_{j=1}^{s} r_{tj}P_{tj}u_{tj}m_{tj}P_{tj} \qquad (6.1)$$

Both sides of equation (6.1) now signify the total income change rather than the average income change.

Aggregating equation (3), the equation that includes the inter-sector activities, in a manner similar to the above we obtain

$$\Delta g_{t+1}P_{t+1} = \sum\limits_{j=1}^{s} (A_{tj} + a_{tj})B_{tj}g_{tj}P_{t+1,j} - \sum\limits_{j=1}^{s} (r_{tj} + R_{tj})P_{tj}u_{tj}P_{t+1,j} \qquad (7)$$

In (7) population size in sector j for period t+1 is $(1+r_{tj} + R_{tj})P_{tj}$ or $(m_{tj} + R_{tj})P_{tj}$. Substituting for $P_{t+1,j}$ we obtain

$$\Delta g_{t+1}P_{t+1} = \sum\limits_{j=1}^{s} (A_{tj}+a_{tj})B_{tj}g_{tj}(m_{tj}+R_{tj})P_{tj} -$$

$$\sum\limits_{j=1}^{s} (r_{tj}+R_{tj})P_{tj}u_{tj}(m_{tj}+R_{tj})P_{tj} \qquad (8)$$

which for our purposes can be rewritten in more convenient form as

$$\Delta g_{t+1} P_{t+1} = \sum_{j=1}^{s} A_{tj} B_{tj} g_{tj} m_{tj} P_{tj} - \sum_{j=1}^{s} r_{tj} P_{tj} u_{tj} m_{tj} P_{tj}$$

(9)

$$+ \sum_{j=1}^{s} a_{tj} B_{tj} g_{tj} m_{tj} P_{tj} + \sum_{j=1}^{s} A_{tj} B_{tj} g_{tj} R_{tj} P_{tj} + \sum_{j=1}^{s} a_{tj} B_{tj} g_{tj} R_{tj} P_{tj}$$

$$- \sum_{j=1}^{s} r_{tj} P_{tj} u_{tj} R_{tj} P_{tj} - \sum_{j=1}^{s} R_{tj} P_{tj} u_{tj} m_{tj} P_{tj} - \sum_{j=1}^{s} R_{tj} P_{tj} u_{tj} R_{tj} P_{tj}$$

Now the first two terms of the right hand side of (9) are identical with equation (6). Assuming that for small changes in investment the value of B_{tj} remains approximately constant, and that for small changes in population the values of u_{tj} remain approximately constant we are in a position to examine equations (9) and (6.1) and determine the change caused by the inter-sector activities. For if B_{tj} and u_{tj} are approximately constant, then the difference that the inter-sector activities make is described by the last six terms on the right hand side of equation (9). Hence we can get some insight into the effects of inter-sector activities if we can give some economic and demographic interpretation to the last six terms of the right side of equation (9).

The first two terms indicate what would have happened had no inter-sector activities taken place. This need not be gone into in any detail since the analysis of the previous chapters takes care of this case. The third term

$$\sum_{j=1}^{s} a_{tj} B_{tj} g_{tj} m_{tj} P_{tj}$$

expresses the effect of the redistribution of investment between sectors. It expresses the addition to the total income change (and to total national income) produced by investment across sector lines. While it is conceivable that the inter-sector investment choices made should be so faulty that

$$\sum_{j=1}^{s} a_{tj} B_{tj} g_{tj} m_{tj} P_{tj}$$

turns out on balance to be negative it is not generally expected to be the case. Given some foresight and calculation, and reasonably rational motivation in choice then

$$\sum_{j=1}^{s} a_{tj} B_{tj} g_{tj} m_{tj} P_{tj}$$

would be expected to be positive.

The fourth term

$$\sum_{j=1}^{s} A_{tj} B_{tj} g_{tj} R_{tj} P_{tj}$$

expresses the net addition to national income increase that would have occurred as a result of the inter-sector population shifts apart from the effects of the simultaneous investment shifts, and also of course apart from losses due to superior or inferior capital-labor ratios. (The effects of diminishing or increasing returns are accounted for by the terms that contain u.) Although this term may be negative we would generally expect it to be positive. That is, we would generally expect population to shift to those areas where investment is taking place and where the average rates of return are higher.[5]

The fifth term

$$\sum_{j=1}^{s} a_{tj} B_{tj} g_{tj} R_{tj} P_{tj}$$

expresses the effect of the simultaneous interaction of the inter-sector investment shifts with the population shifts. This term is likely to

---

[5] Of course other combinations of investment and population shifts are possible. In the next section some of the effects of other possible patterns of investment and population shifts are considered. See especially Table III, below.

be positive if the population shifts have been in the same direction as the investment shifts and negative if they have not. For some sectors the population shifts result in a net addition to the sector population size and for others in a net subtraction. If the sectors which gain people also gain capital and the sectors which lose people also lose capital then the fifth term must be positive, since, in this case, $a_{tj}B_{tj}g_{tj}R_{tj}P_{tj}$ will be positive for all sectors. For any sector the expression $a_{tj}B_{tj}g_{tj}R_{tj}P_{tj}$ will be negative only where a_{tj} and R_{tj} are of opposite sign.

The interpretation of the last three terms is somewhat more difficult than the previous three. The last three terms taken together represent the total change in the diminution in income due to the operation of decreasing (and increasing) returns effected by the population shifts. Now, in working with portions of the total national income change the population shifts affect the magnitudes of the last three terms in two ways. First, within a sector an increase (decrease) in population requires that the u_{tj}'s be multiplied by a greater (lesser) amount in order to get the average income loss for the sector as a whole, since u_{tj} is the average income loss per unit of population. Second, to get the total income loss for the sector that is due to diminishing returns it is necessary to multiply the average income loss for the sector again by the population size of the sector which in turn is affected by the population shift.

Roughly speaking, the sixth term

$$\sum_{j=1}^{s} r_{tj}P_{tj}u_{tj}R_{tj}P_{tj}$$

represents the addition to the original total income loss due to the population increase; that is, it represents the original average loss $r_{tj}P_{tj}u_{tj}$ for each sector multiplied by the population shift in each sector.

However, the original average income loss $(r_{tj}P_{tj}u_{tj})$ is no longer applicable in view of the population shifts. Term seven accounts for the total income loss due to the population shifts on the basis of the sectors' old population sizes, while term eight accounts for the change in the sectors' population sizes.

It is really quite difficult to give a clear-cut verbal interpretation of equation (9). It might help to clarify matters if we consider a diagrammatical representation of a typical sector's contribution to the total income increase. The contribution that sector j
makes to the total income increase is expressed in equation (10).

$$\Delta g_{t+1,j} P_{t+1,j} = A_{tj} B_{tj} g_{tj} m_{tj} P_{tj} - r_{tj} P_{tj} u_{tj} m_{tj} P_{tj}$$

$$+ a_{tj} B_{tj} g_{tj} m_{tj} P_{tj} + A_{tj} B_{tj} g_{tj} R_{tj} P_{tj} + a_{tj} B_{tj} g_{tj} R_{tj} P_{tj}$$

$$- r_{tj} P_{tj} u_{tj} R_{tj} P_{tj} - R_{tj} P_{tj} u_{tj} m_{tj} P_{tj} - R_{tj} P_{tj} u_{tj} R_{tj} P_{tj}$$

$$(10)$$

The right hand side of this equation is of course identical with the right
hand side of equation (9), except for the summation signs. Fig. 9 is a
diagrammatical representation of the right hand side of equation (10).
        The two rectangles represent the total income increase
due to investment and the income loss due to the increase in numbers.
The numbers inside the smaller rectangles each refer to the term
that the rectangle represents. Thus, the rectangle marked (3) represents the third term on the right side of equation (10). Let us consider
each of the larger rectangles separately.
        Left rectangle. This rectangle is made up of four small-
er rectangles which represent the four terms in which investment is
involved.
        (1) This rectangle represents the increase in national
income that would have occurred had there been no population increase
and neither inter-sector investment shifts nor population shifts. It is
constructed as follows: The amount of average investment is measured
along the abscissa. This amount is $A_{tj} g_{tj}$. The average income-average investment ratio (B_{tj}) is represented by the small portion on the
ordinate that is so designated. Thus, the little rectangle marked
$A_{tj} B_{tj} g_{tj}$ represents the increase in average income that would have
taken place had there been neither population changes nor inter-sector
investment shifts. Now, the increase in average income has to be multiplied by the population of the sector to obtain the increase in total income for the sector. Population size is measured along the ordinate.

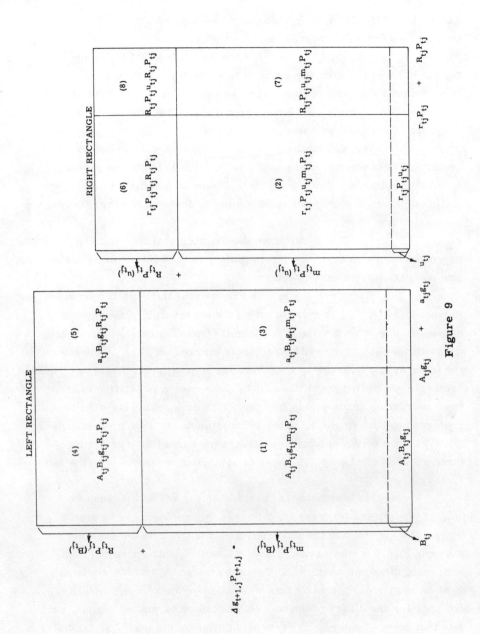

Figure 9

The little rectangle $A_{tj}B_{tj}g_{tj}$ has to be multiplied by $m_{tj}P_{tj}$ to obtain the rectangle that represents $A_{tj}B_{tj}g_{tj}m_{tj}P_{tj}$.

(3) This rectangle represents the effect of the net increase in investment on the sector's total income. The net addition to investment that comes from other sectors is marked on the abscissa as an addition to the intra-sector investment. The size of this rectangle is determined as above.

(4) The addition to the sector's population due to inter-sector shifts is plotted on the ordinate as an addition to the sector's original population. Multiplying the increase in population due to population shifts by the original increase in the sector's average income we obtain term four.

(5) It is clear from the diagram that this rectangle represents the simultaneous interaction of the receipt of investment and population from other sectors.

Right rectangle. (2) The natural intra-sector increase in population $(r_{tj}P_{tj})$ is marked off on the abcissa. The average income loss due to an increase in one unit of population (u_{tj}) is marked off on the ordinate. The little rectangle marked $r_{tj}P_{tj}u_{tj}$ represents the intra-sector average income loss due to population increase. This rectangle multiplied by what would be the sector's population apart from population shifts yields rectangle (2). Now, using the approach analogous to that employed in the left rectangle we develop rectangles (6), (7) and (8). We need not go through the verbal interpretation of these rectangles since the scheme is analogous to that used in the left rectangle.

We may note that rectangles (3), (4) and (5) less rectangles (6), (7) and (8), represent the net income increase to sector j that can be ascribed to the inter-sector activities. In the example shown in Fig. 9 it was assumed that a_{tj} and R_{tj} are positive. But, of course, for some sectors a_{tj} must be negative, and for some R_{tj} must be negative. In those cases where either or both a_{tj} and R_{tj} are negative the diagrammatical representation is just as simple, except that some of the rectangles would be inside others. For example, if R_{tj} is negative then rectangle (4) would be inside rectangle (1) illustrating a deduction from (1) rather than an addition.

The Basic Identity, Equilibrium Conditions, and
Stability Conditions

The basic identity does not by itself explain the course
of average income over time. In order to understand the course of
average income over time it would be necessary to know the factors
that determine $A_{tj}, a_{tj}, r_{tj}, R_{tj}, B_{tj}, u_{tj}$, for all sectors. Or at least
we would have to postulate a model that explains the determination of
the variables indicated. An extensive analysis of the stability or instability of the multi-sector system probably cannot be made without
the construction of models of such a high degree of complexity and
containing so many variables that it would be exceedingly difficult
(if not impossible) to manipulate the equations in order to deduce the
stability conditions. However, some remarks of a heuristic nature
can be made about the equilibrium and stability of the system on the
basis of what has been said heretofore. The discussion that follows is
intended to be, as it perforce must be, only of a rough and suggestive
nature.

The equilibrium conditions. In a multi-sector system
a condition of general equilibrium exists if in each sector the determinants of the magnitudes of the variables are such that without displacements the variables persist at the same level period after period.
It is conceivable that for each model posited the equilibrium conditions
are different. It appears that without delineating the details of the
model it is not possible to determine the necessary equilibrium conditions but it may be possible to indicate a set of equilibrium conditions that are sufficient.

Now, on the basis of equation (9) we can say that a
sufficient equilibrium condition is the following. Namely, the system
is in equilibrium if $a_{tj}, A_{tj}, r_{tj}, R_{tj}$, are all equal to zero, for all j,
when g_{tj} is zero. This condition says that there exists in each sector a level of average income that would induce neither net investment,
population growth, net capital shifts, nor population shifts. It implies
that if at equilibrium there exist differentials in average income between sectors then these differentials are not sufficient to induce either
net capital movements or net population movements. Thus, it is not a
necessary condition of equilibrium that average income be equal in all
sectors. The equilibrium condition just described is in conformity

with the equilibrium conditions stated in earlier portions of this essay, and hence are useful as points of departure.

Some remarks on the stability of the system. In considering the stability of the system in the context of a multi-sector model the major consideration is the extent to which the inter-sector events raise or depress average income. The major events considered are the population shifts and the investment shifts. The meaning of a population shift is obvious; it refers to the extent to which net in- or out-migration has taken place between any two sectors within a unit period. By an investment shift we refer to the extent to which net savings that occur in one sector are invested in another.

The initial income raising effects of the investment shifts depend on the B's; that is, roughly speaking on the incremental average income-incremental average investment ratios. The greater the gap in the B's between the sectors from which investment comes and those to which investment goes (assuming the B's are higher in those sectors receiving investment than in those in which the savings took place) the greater the initial income raising effects of the investment shifts. However, in the long run this is not necessarily the case. For future average income growth depends in part on the proportions of income saved in the various sectors. Thus the long run average income raising effects of investment shifts may be furthered by shifting investment to sectors where the B's are not quite as high as others but where the proportions saved out of the average income gains are sufficiently greater. Also, the effect of population increases on average income must not be neglected in considering investment shifts. It follows that, other things equal, capital growth will be the greater if investment flows to those sectors where the detrimental effects of the population increases on the average income gains are least.

The income raising effects of the population shifts also depend on a number of factors. The initial income raising effects will depend on: (1) the direction of the population flows, (2) the original gap in average incomes between sectors receiving population and those losing it, and (3) the gaps in the u's between sectors receiving population and those losing it. It is assumed that those entering into a sector receive on the average the same income as those already in it.

Hence, the effect of the population shift into the sector is determined
by the magnitude of the shift and the value of u for that sector. A
population shift from a sector where average income is lower to one
where it is higher will, up to some magnitude of the population movement, increase average income. To gauge the ultimate effect of the
population redistribution an additional consideration must be made;
namely, the gaps in fertility and mortality rates between the various
sectors from which population is coming and those to which it is
going. This of course will depend in part on the extent to which the
shifting population takes on the fertility and mortality characteristics
of the sectors into which it enters. In any event it is obvious that
these are considerations to be taken into account.

       From what has been said it is clear that the effects of
the inter-sector events depend, in part, on the pattern of investment
and population shifts that take place period after period. But the difficulty for analysis is that the possible patterns of inter-sector events
are almost infinite. It is conceivable that in some cases a portion of
the population will shift from sectors where average income is high to
those where it is low, while in other portions of the economy the reverse will take place. Similarly, savings created in sectors where incomes are low may become investment in sectors where incomes are
high, and vice versa. Also, investment and population may shift, in
part, either from sectors where the B's are high to where they are
low, and in part in the reverse direction. A similar possibility exists
with respect to the u's. With a reasonably large number of sectors
the number of possible combinations becomes exceedingly large.

       To make some headway without trying to do the im-
possible -- namely, to consider a large or infinite number of possible
cases -- we can make some assumptions about the nature of the investment and population shifts so that the number of possible combinations
is considerably reduced. It is this that is attempted below.

       Now, in order to make some rudimentary comparisons
between the aggregative and multi-sector ways of looking at the economy we should note that we can regard the aggregative model in two ways.
(1) We can assume that each sector operates in isolation and that the
aggregative model represents the simple addition of the results a-
chieved in each sector. In other words, we regard the aggregative model

as one in which inter-sector activities do not occur. We are enabled thereby to compare the situation in which inter-sector activities do not occur with the situation in which they do. (2) The second possibility is to assume that the aggregative model takes into account the inter-sector activities and to raise the question: How do the inter-sector activities affect the magnitudes of the aggregative variables?

First, then, let us consider a limited number of investment and population flow patterns. We differentiate between four possible types of investment and population shifts. These are as follows:

I. Both investment and population shifts from sectors where average income is lower to sectors where average income is higher.

II. Both investment and population shifts from sectors where average income is higher to sectors where average income is lower.

III. Investment shifts to sectors where average income is lower while population shifts to sectors where average income is higher.

IV. Investment shifts to sectors where average income is higher while population shifts to sectors where average income is lower.

Now, within each type of investment and population shift considered above we differentiate between four possible distributions of the B's and u's among the various sectors. These are:

(a) The B's are higher where average income is higher, while the u's are lower in those sectors where average income is higher.

(b) The B's are higher in those sectors where average income is higher, while the u's are higher where average income is higher.

(c) The B's are lower in those sectors where average income is higher, while the u's are higher where average income is higher.

(d) The B's are lower in those sectors where average income is higher, while the u's are lower in those sectors where average income is higher.

This two-way classification yields sixteen possible

patterns or combinations of population and investment shifts and of
the distribution of the B's and u's among the various sectors. This
limited number of patterns is obtained, of course, at the expense of
ignoring all "mixed cases"; that is, those situations in which neither
all of the population moves are in the same direction, from low to high
average incomes or vice versa, nor are all the investment shifts in
the same direction. In part of some of the analysis that follows a factor of some significance is the propensity to save in the various sectors. We shall assume as before that savings are a monotonic increasing function of income. Thus, average savings are higher in
those sectors where average income is higher.

     Now, the effects of the inter-sector events depend on
the specific pattern of investment and population shifts. Given the sixteen patterns delineated above we can compare some of the patterns
in various ways with each other and see which patterns are likely to
have the highest income raising effects, which the lowest, and in which
cases the effects are indeterminate. The results of such comparisons
are summarized in Table III. The remarks above the diagonal in Table
III are the results of the comparison of the income raising effects for
a given type of investment and population shift with respect to the four
different distributions of the B's and u's considered. That is, I(a),
I(b), I(c), and I(d) are compared with each other; similarly II(a), II(b),
II(c), and II(d) are compared with each other; and so on. The remarks
below the diagonal in each square signify the results obtained when
comparing the four different patterns of investment and population
shifts for the different given distributions of the B's and u's. That
is, the remarks below the diagonal refer to the "vertical" rather than
to the "horizontal" comparisons in Table III.

     Consider cases I(a), I(b), I(c), and I(d). That is, con-
sider those situations in which both population and investment move
from sectors in which average income is lower to sectors where average income is higher. Casual examination indicates that I(a) is likely
to be most income raising, I(c) is likely to be least income raising,
and that I(b) and I(d) are likely to be in between, that is, worse than
I(a) but better than I(c). Compare for a moment I(a) and I(c). In
I(a) investment flows to sectors where the B's are higher, and other

things equal, average income will be higher than in I(c) where investment flows to the sectors where the B's are lower. Simultaneously,
in pattern I(a) population flows to sectors where the u's are lower
while the reverse happens under pattern I(c), and as a consequence
the population shift helps to increase average income in I(a) while it
reduces it in I(c).

Whether pattern I(b) is better or worse than I(c) cannot be determined a priori. In these two situations the investment and
population shifts have opposite effects. Under I(b) the investment
shifts have income raising effects because investment flows to sectors
where the B's are higher, but at the same time the population shifts
have, in part, income dampening effects because the u's are higher
in the sectors to which population gravitates. Exactly the opposite
situation holds under I(d). Without a fuller specification of the magnitudes of the variables involved patterns I(b) and I(d) cannot be compared and ranked with respect to their income raising effects.

The other three "horizontal" groups of four patterns
each can be compared in a similar manner. In view of the analogous
nature of the comparisons it is probably not necessary to go through
the details of each of them at this point. (The interested reader can
do that for himself if he wishes.) The results of such comparisons are
indicated in the appropriate squares above the diagonal line in Table III.

The "vertical" comparisons (i.e. comparing I(a), II(a),
III(a), and IV(a) with each other, and so on) are somewhat more difficult to make and in general the results are somewhat less determinate.
With respect to each pattern there are four effects to consider. These
are:

(1) The effect on average income of the investment shift
to sectors where the B's are higher rather than lower, or vice versa.

(2) The secondary effect on average income of the investment shift to sectors where a greater or lesser proportion of income is saved.

(3) The effect on average income of the population shift
to sectors where the u's are lower, or vice versa.

(4) The second effect on average income of the population shift to sectors where average income is higher than in those sectors from which the population comes, or vice versa.

Consider the first group of investment and population shift patterns, (i.e. I(a), II(a), III(a), and IV(a).) In this comparison, if we assume that the distribution of the B's and u's is fixed, it is clear that pattern I is better than any of the others, if we consider only the four effects just outlined. Under pattern I all of the effects are average income raising. Under none of the other patterns is this necessarily true. Considering each of the four effects in turn we find that under pattern I investment moves from sectors where the B's are lower to those where the B's are higher, and as a consequence average income is raised to a higher level than it would be if the investment shifts did not take place. Out of a higher average income the proportion saved and invested is higher, potential average income growth is therefore greater, and hence there is a gain with respect to the second effect considered. Population moves from sectors where the u's are higher to those where the u's are lower, and as a result average income is in this case higher than it would be if the population shifts did not take place. At the same time population moves from sectors where average income is lower to those where average income is higher. Given our assumption that workers entering a sector receive on the average the same wage as those already in the sector then average income will also be raised on this account under pattern I. This implies, of course, that under pattern I the size of the population shift is not so large that it depresses wages in the sector into which it enters and raises wages in the sector out of which the population comes to such an extent that in the end average income in the sector gaining population is lower than the average income in the sector losing people. Examining pattern II in the same manner that we have just examined pattern I shows that all of the four effects are in this case average income dampening as compared to the situation in which the investment and population shifts do not take place. All in all it seems that pattern I most likely represents the best situation of the four considered, pattern II most likely represents the worst, and patterns III and IV are most likely in between. The word likely is used because in part the end result depends on the extent of the shifts that take place between sectors.

As before no attempt is made at this point to go into

TABLE III

SUMMARY OF COMPARISONS OF THE EFFECTS OF DIFFERENT PATTERNS
OF INVESTMENT AND POPULATION SHIFTS

Horizontal Comparisons / Vertical Comparisons	(a) The B's are higher where average income is higher, and the u's are lower where average income is higher.	(b) The B's are higher where average income is higher, and the u's are higher where average income is higher.	(c) The B's are lower where average income is higher, and the u's are higher where average income is higher.	(d) The B's are lower where average income is higher, and the u's are lower where average income is higher.
I. Both Investment and Population shift to sectors where average income is higher.	Best / Best (1) Gain* (2) Gain (3) Gain (4) Gain	In between / ? (1) Gain (2) Gain (3) Loss (4) Gain	Worst / ? (1) Loss (2) Gain (3) Loss (4) Gain	In between / ? (1) Loss (2) Gain (3) Gain (4) Gain
II. Both Investment and Population shift to sectors where average income is lower.	Worst / Worst (1) Loss (2) Loss (3) Loss (4) Loss	In between / ? (1) Loss (2) Loss (3) Gain (4) Loss	Best / ? (1) Gain (2) Loss (3) Gain (4) Loss	In between / ? (1) Gain (2) Loss (3) Loss (4) Loss
III. Investment shifts to sectors where average income is lower. -- Population shifts to sectors where average income is higher.	In between / ? (1) Loss (2) Loss (3) Gain (4) Gain	Worst / ? (1) Loss (2) Loss (3) Loss (4) Gain	In between / ? (1) Gain (2) Loss (3) Loss (4) Gain	Best / ? (1) Gain (2) Loss (3) Gain (4) Gain
IV. Investment shifts to sectors where average income is higher. -- Population shifts to sectors where average income is lower.	In between / ? (1) Gain (2) Gain (3) Loss (4) Loss	Best / ? (1) Gain (2) Gain (3) Gain (4) Loss	In between / ? (1) Loss (2) Gain (3) Gain (4) Loss	Worst / ? (1) Loss (2) Gain (3) Loss (4) Loss

EXPLANATION OF REMARKS BELOW DIAGONAL:

In each square the four numbers identify each of the four effects listed below. The word "gain" beside a number indicates that average income for the economy is likely to be higher under the specified pattern of investment and population shifts than the average income would be if the investment and population shifts did not take place, if we take into account only the effect under consideration. The word "loss" beside the number of the effect being considered indicates that under the specified shifts average income is likely to be lower than it would be if the sectors operated in isolation. The four effects considered are as follows:

(1) The effect on average income of the investment shift to sectors where the B's are higher rather than lower, or vice versa.
(2) The secondary effect on average income of the investment shift to sectors where a greater as against a lesser proportion of income is saved, or vice versa.
(3) The effect on average income of the population shift to sectors where the u's are lower, or vice versa.
(4) The second effect on average income of the population shift to sectors where average income is higher than in those sectors from which the population comes, or vice versa.

the details of all the other comparisons possible. In all cases the
method of comparison is analogous to the one just indicated. Some of
the results are summarized in Table III. The reader will note however
that in most of the squares there is a question mark below the diagonal
in Table III. The reason for this is that in most cases some of the
effects are average income raising while others are average income
dampening as compared with the situation in which the investment and
population shifts do not take place. However, the nature of the four
effects is noted under each case. In each square in Table III the words
"gain" and "loss" after a given number show whether under the
pattern in question the effect that is indicated by the number is likely
to be income raising or income dampening. It is likely that by making
various assumptions about the importance of different effects a more
determinate ranking of the alternate patterns of investment and population shifts can be achieved.

Now, in view of what has been said, let us see if we can
relate in any way our discussion of the multi-sector model with the
conclusions arrived at in our outline of the aggregative model in Chapter IV. In conformity with the previously postulated models we assume
at first that A_{tj} and r_{tj} are up to some values of g_{tj} monotonic increasing functions of g_{tj}, and that beyond these values of g_{tj} both
A_{tj} and r_{tj} take on maximum values. If the magnitudes of the B's
and the u's are constant or approximately constant over time then we
have a situation that is analogous to the simple dynamic model outlined
in Chapter IV. In addition to the postulates already made we have to
say something about the pattern of investment and population shifts
that is to be assumed. We consider at the outset pattern I(a). As already indicated under this pattern the investment and population shifts
help to raise average income to a level above what it would be without
them. However the average income raising effects of the investment
shifts are limited by the amount of total investment in any period. Even
if in each period investment is always allocated between sectors in an
optimum manner (i.e. optimum from the point of view of raising average income) the total income raising effects of the investment shifts
have an upper bound determined by the magnitude of investment. Similarly the extent of the population shifts possible within any period has
an upper bound and as a consequence the income raising effect of the

population shifts has a maximum. These upper bounds of the income
raising effects of investment and population shifts are determined, as
previously indicated, by the gaps between sectors in the magnitudes
of the B's, by the gaps between sectors in the magnitudes of the u's,
and by the extent of the shifts themselves. It must also be recognized
that beyond some point the population shifts can go too far. As long
as the u's in all sectors have some positive value then the population
shifts decrease average income in those sectors where population
enters and increase it in those sectors from where population departs.
The optimum population shifts within any period, if our criterion is
the maximization of income during that period, are those that result
in an equalization of average incomes in all sectors. Thus it is clear
that the income raising effects of the population shifts must have an
upper bound. (If population really shifts to those sectors where average income is higher then population will stop shifting once inter-sector equalization of average incomes is achieved.) In view of these
facts we have a situation similar to that considered in Chapter IV.
Thus, the analysis and conclusions of Chapter IV are with some modifications applicable to this case. Specifically, if on the average the
maximum A's are greater than the maximum r's then the system is
likely to be stable for small displacements and unstable for large ones.

However, it is important to note that according to the
first means of comparing the multi-sector and aggregative models one
of the conclusions arrived at in Chapter IV does not necessarily hold.
If the aggregative model represents the situation in which the sectors
operate in isolation, and if on the average the maximum r's are
greater than the maximum A's then the system is not necessarily
stable for all displacements. It may happen that the income raising
effects of the investment and population shifts may be so great as to
be sufficient to destabilize the system. That is to say, the investment
and population shifts can lead to a situation in which the maximum
(A+a)'s are greater than the maximum (r+R)'s although the maximum A's are less than the maximum r's.

If the assumed relationships between the r_{tj}'s and the
g_{tj}'s are such that beyond some magnitudes of g_{tj} the value of r_{tj}
declines then we have a situation similar to the conditions considered
in the early part of Chapter VI. Via analogous reasoning it can be

shown that the conclusions of Chapter VI are also applicable to the
multi-sector model if the pattern of investment and population shifts
is of the type described under I(a). However, reference to Table III
indicates that some patterns of investment and population shifts are
income dampening rather than average income raising when compared
to the situation under which the sectors operate in isolation. In such
cases the results of Chapters IV and VI need not apply for the system
may be unstable when the sectors are considered in isolation (for a
given displacement or set of displacements) but the system may be
stable when the inter-sector activities are taken into account.

It is probably a more sensible procedure to interpret
the aggregative models not as situations in which the sectors operate
in isolation but more realistically as aggregations of those situations
in which inter-sector activities do take place. What light does our
consideration of inter-sector activities throw on such models? In a
broad sense the extent to which the system is stable depends on the
extent to which the endogenous events generated by an exogenous shock
are average income raising or average income depressing. Therefore,
to the extent to which a consideration of the different possible patterns
of the investment and population shifts (and the concommitant distribution of B's and u's) tells us something about the different income
raising (or depressing) effects of these patterns, we have additional
insight into the effects of the inter-sector activities on the stability
of the system. A study of Table III reveals that some patterns of inter-
sector activities are distinctly better than others; e.g. pattern I(a)
is more likely to lead to the instability of the system than one that
approximates II(a). Other comparisons of a similar nature can probably be made so that additional light may be thrown on the problem of
determining the likelihood of a given displacement being stable or
unstable.

APPENDIX TO CHAPTER VII

Outline of a Specific Multi-Sector Model

Probably the most direct way of showing the relationship between the basic identity (equation (9)) and multi-sector model construction is to set up a model that employs equation (9) effectively. Unfortunately, given the state of our empirical knowledge about the relationship between demographic and economic variables, we find that we can suggest a large variety of models. We do not know the determinants of many of the factors that we are concerned with and hence all that can be done is to indicate some of the possibilities, of which there are many. Nevertheless it may be useful to outline a possible model even though the behavior equations postulated are mere guesses. Such an example can serve as an illustration of the type of thing that could be done if the empirical information were available. It also may suggest some of the things to look for in empirical work.

If we are given the values of A_{tj}, a_{tj}, B_{tj}, r_{tj}, R_{tj}, and u_{tj}, for all j, then we could employ equation (9) to compute the change in average income that takes place between two successive periods. Also, we could employ equation (10) to determine the same thing for any specific sector. Hence, any model that permits the determination of A_{tj}, a_{tj}, B_{tj}, r_{tj}, R_{tj}, and u_{tj} will permit the determination of the course of average income over time. Our task therefore is to suggest a model that determines the values of the variables just stated. For the initial period we are given the g_{tj}'s, and hence the average incomes for each sector. Our initial conditions also include the population size of each sector, the age distribution of the population, and the capital initially available in each sector. For ease in exposition let us assume that each sector represents a different industry; or, more accurately, each sector is made up of the group whose livelihood arises out of a particular industry. We further assume that nobody's source

132

of livelihood stems from more than one industry. Also, for some of
our relationships it will be convenient to divide up the industry sectors by age groupings.

      1. One of the ways of determining A_{tj} is to determine
first the demand functions for the various consumer goods, which in
turn will permit us to determine total expenditures for consumer goods,
at given prices. Knowing total expenditures on consumer goods we
readily determine average expenditures. Average income less average expenditures yields average savings, which readily leads to the
determination of A_{tj}.

      Our first set of functions are the demand functions:

(11.1) $$_kD_{tjx} = {}_kF_{tjx}(\bar{p}_{t1} \cdots, \bar{p}_{tk}, \cdots, \bar{p}_{ts}, y_{tjx})$$

$$(k = 1,2,\ldots,s)$$
$$(j = 1,2,\ldots,s)$$

where $_kD_{tjx}$ = the average quantity of commodity k demanded by
those in sector j and age group x. The average quantity is simply
the total quantity demanded divided by the number in the sector and
age group considered. The s prices of the s commodities made in the
the s sectors are designated by $\bar{p}_{t1},\ldots,\bar{p}_{ts}$; and the average income
for the sector and age group is designated by y_{tjx}. Let P_{tjx} be the
population of sector j age group x. Total expenditure on consumer
goods and services made by those in sector j is given by the expression

$$\sum_k \sum_x {}_kD_{tjx}\bar{P}_{tk}P_{tjx}$$

and it follows that A_{tj} is given by:

$$A_{tj} = \frac{\dfrac{y_{tj}P_{tj} - \sum_k \sum_x {}_kD_{tjx}\bar{P}_{tk}P_{tjx}}{P_{tj}}}{g_{tj}}$$

which can be computed for all j.[6]

It is generally recognized that the age group people are in and their occupational grouping will affect their consumption habits. By using age-specific and sector-specific demand functions we are able to account for the effects of the age distribution and occupational distribution of the population on demand. The reason for using average rather than total demand functions is explained later.

2. The above equations permit the determination of the total funds available for investment. However, they do not tell us what the distribution of investment between sectors will be. Unfortunately, not very much is known about the determinants of investment. Let us assume that the amount invested in a given sector depends on the total funds available for investment, and on the quantities demanded of the goods produced in the different sectors. We therefore write the s investment functions for the s sectors

$$I_{tk} = f_{tk}(_1D_t, \ldots, {_k}D_t, \ldots, {_s}D_t, I_t)$$

$$(k = 1, \ldots, s)$$

(11.2)

where the total quantity demanded of commodity k is written

$${_k}D_t = \sum_k \sum_x {_k}D_{tjx}$$

and where the total funds available for investment are designated by

$$I_t = \sum_j y_{tj}P_{tj} - \sum_k {_k}D_t \bar{p}_{tk}.$$

I_{tk} represents the amount invested in sector k. We can now compute a_{tj}, for all j, by the formula

$$a_{tj} = \frac{I_{tj} - A_{tj}g_{tj}}{g_{tj}}$$

---

[6]   One of the reasons for using this roundabout way of determining savings by postulating the demand functions first is that the total quantities demanded of each commodity are necessary for the determination of commodity prices.

3. The B_{tj}'s depend on the technical nature of the capital employed in each of the industries, on the nature and amount of the investment, and on the relative prices for which goods exchange. We shall assume that the technical nature of the capital used in each sector is given. Prices for commodities are determined by demand and supply conditions. We therefore write the functions that determine the B_{tj}'s as follows:

(11.3) $$B_{tj} = \bar{f}_{tj}(I_{tj}, \bar{P}_{t1}, \ldots, \bar{P}_{ts})$$

$$(j = 1,2,\ldots,s).$$

4. The r_{tj}'s depend on the initial age distribution of the population for each sector, and on the age-specific fertility rates, and the age-specific mortality rates. We assume that age-specific fertility rates and age-specific mortality rates within each sector are functions of average income. We therefore write this set of functions as

(11.4) $$r_{tj} = F_{tj}(P_{tj}, \ldots, P_{tjx}, \ldots, y_{tj})$$

$$(j = 1,2,\ldots,s).$$

5. In order to determine the R_{tj}'s a theory of population mobility and labor mobility is necessary. We shall assume here that the proportion of any age group within a sector that moves from one sector to another is determined by the cost of movement between sectors, and by the relative opportunities in the various sectors as reflected by the comparative average incomes between the sectors. We represent this relationship by

(11.5) $$_k L_{tjx} = Q_{tjx}(_k \bar{C}_j, y_{t1}, \ldots, y_{tj}, \ldots, y_{ts})$$

$$(k = 1,2,\ldots,s)$$

$$(j = 1,2,\ldots,s)$$

where $_k L_{tjx}$ is the proportion of those aged x in sector k that leave for sector j. $_k \bar{C}_j$ stands for the cost of moving from sector k to sector j. (The cost of moving can either be assumed to be given, or it can be computed on the basis of the prices charged by those sectors that provide moving services.) Let us write E_{tj} for the number that enter sector j from other sectors and L_{tj} for the number that leave sector j for other sectors. The number leaving sector j, and the number entering sector j are computed as follows:

$$E_{tj} = \sum_k \sum_x {}_kL_{tjx}P_{tkx}$$

$$L_{tj} = \sum_s \sum_x {}_jL_{tsx}P_{tjx}$$

And from these we obtain the R_{tj}'s by

$$R_{tj} = \frac{E_{tj} - L_{tj}}{P_{tj}}$$

6. The u_{tj}'s are determined by the technical nature of the capital, the amount of investment, and the increment in population. As before the technical nature of the capital is assumed to be given. Hence we write these functions as follows:

$$u_{tj} = \Psi_{tj}[I_{tj}, (r_{tj} + R_{tj})P_{tj}]$$

$$(j = 1,2,\ldots,s). \qquad\qquad (11.6)$$

7. The set of prices for the commodities are determined by the quantities demanded of the various commodities, and on the supply of the factors that produce these commodities. The supply of labor depends on the size of the population within the sector and on its age distribution. The supply of other factors depends on the capital available within the sector, and on the prices of all other goods that can be used as raw materials. We may write this function as

$$\bar{P}_{tj} = \Phi_{tj}({}_1D_t, \ldots, {}_sD_t, P_{tj1}, \ldots, P_{tjx}, \ldots, P_{tjx}, \ldots,$$

$$\bar{P}_t, \ldots, \bar{P}_{tj-1}, \bar{P}_{tj+1}, \ldots, \bar{P}_{ts}, K_{tj}) \qquad (11.7)$$

(K_{tj} stands for capital in sector j.) Of course, other functions that attempt to explain price determination are possible.

If the functions postulated above were known, then the system of equations stated above would give us the values for the parameters employed in equation (9). This in turn would permit the determination of the change in average income between period t and period t+1, and also the determination of average income in period t+1. Similarly, equation (10) would permit the determination of the average income for each of the sectors. If the functions are assumed to be stable over time then we can determine the course of average income over time. Knowing the age-specific and sector-specific mortality and fertility rates for period t, and knowing the age-specific sector-specific population shifts for period t we can determine the size of each age group in each sector for period t+1. This last in addition to the average age-specific sector-specific demand functions will permit the determination of the total demand functions in period t+1. From here we can continue as before to determine the change in average income between period t+1 and period t+2 -- and so on for any number of periods we may be interested in.

CHAPTER VIII

ON THE CONSTRUCTION OF
MICRO-ECONOMIC-DEMOGRAPHIC THEORIES

I

In economics we usually think of micro-economic theories as theories based on individual behavior, while macro-economic
theories deal with aggregates of individuals. (For ease in exposition
we shall omit the adjectives "economic-demographic" in our discussions. We shall refer to the type of theories considered in the
previous chapters as macro-theories, and to theories that begin with
individual behavior as micro-theories.) At the present time macro-
theories are probably more useful than micro-theories. The reasons
for this are not difficult to find. Theories involving higher levels of
aggregation usually contain fewer equations than those on lower levels
of aggregation and as a consequence are easier to handle. For example, to apply to a modern economic problem a micro-theory of the
Walrasian general equilibrium type would involve obtaining the parameters for and solving a system containing millions of equations. But
even though a micro-theory cannot be used directly in the solution of
practical problems it may still be very useful from a heuristic standpoint.

For a fuller understanding of aggregative phenomena
it is desirable and necessary to understand the behavior of the individual components of the aggregates. This is especially true in those
cases where the theories are in the early stages of development. It
is conceivable and indeed likely that the development of a micro-theory
(or theories) may be useful in the improvement of the counterpart
macro-theory (or theories). Furthermore, we usually have some knowledge of micro-behavior and if our macro-theory is to make sense it

138

is desirable that we be able to square our fragmentary micro knowledge with our macro-theory. In view of this it may be useful to consider the construction of a set of interrelated concepts that can be
employed in the development of micro-theories which in turn can be
related to the macro-theories developed in the previous chapters.

This is not to suggest that in this chapter an attempt
will be made to expound a full-fledged micro-economic-demographic
theory. (This would be much too ambitious an undertaking at this
stage.) Rather, what will be attempted is a presentation and discussion of some of the primary concepts and elements out of which
such micro-economic-demographic theories can be developed.

The Rules of Selection in Economic Theories

At times, it may be expedient and economical to devel-
op a theory along the lines of another theory in a closely related field.
If a theory of demographic-economic change is to be developed along
the lines of existing economic theory then it is relevant to ask whether
there are some analogues in economic theory that can be utilized
fruitfully. It may therefore be of interest to examine certain features
of economic theories and see to what extent, if any, they may be
carried over into the type of theoretical development in which we are
interested.

Micro-economic theory is concerned, in part, with the
problem of choosing between alternatives, and with aggregating the
consequences of the specific choices made by the individual economic
actors. In order to indicate how the specific choice between alternatives is determined micro-economic theories usually posit a maximization principle of some sort. Given the alternatives with which
each of the economic actors is confronted, those in the role of consumers choose in such a way as to attempt to maximize their utilities, while those in the role of sellers of factors of production, or those
in the role of entrepreneurs, attempt to maximize their incomes.

In macro-economic theory of the Keynesian variety the
situation is rather mixed. Whereas wage earners are assumed to
maximize their money incomes and entrepreneurs are assumed to
maximize profits, it is not at all clear how the individual consumer is
assumed to behave. Instead, the theory posits that the aggregate outcome of the individual choices by consumers will be such as to result

in a unique distribution between expenditures on consumer goods and savings for every level of national income. In other words, the theory posits a statistical law about the outcome of consumers' choices but has nothing to say about the rule of selection between alternatives confronting individual consumers.[1]

We thus see that in economic theory, where there is a rule of selection between alternatives, it is a maximization principle of some sort. Where there is no explicit rule of selection between alternatives, as in some aspects of macro-economic theory, it is only possible to by-pass such a rule by positing a relationship between the outcome of individual choices and some other global variable. This is not to imply that writers in economic theory are always aware that in positing a maximization principle they are merely describing a possible rule of selection between alternatives, but essentially it is nothing more than that.[2]

At this point we raise the question whether a maximization principle is suitable for demographic-economic models. It may be that for some sets of alternatives in which economic considerations are paramount a maximization principle may be an adequate rule of selection which may serve as a first approximation. But it would appear that in these situations that are significant in determining changes in fertility and family size a rule of selection which can account for more considerations than the maximization of an economic index is desirable. Certainly there are many cases in which human values (or social norms) do play a role in the determination of decisions that lead to changes in fertility and family size. In view of this a rule of selection that would not account for such factors would appear to be inadequate. Furthermore, if the attempt to maximize something or other does enter into the decision-making process in this area then nothing is really lost if we add systems of values or

---

[1] Here may lie one of the difficulties in integrating micro- and macro-economic theories. Namely, the question arises whether such a simple and at the same time ambiguous and non-operational rule of selection as the maximization of utilities is consistent, under all circumstances, with the current formulation of the consumption function.

[2] This point has been made by Prof. Kenneth E. Boulding. See his article "Professor Tarshis and the State of Economics," _American Economic Review_, Vol. 38, No. 1 (March, 1948), pp. 93 ff.

mores to our description of the rules of selection between alternatives. In view of this we shall consider first the problem of describing a system of values or mores. More specifically, an attempt will be made: (a) to suggest a definition of a value system; (b) to indicate what constitutes the elements of such a system, and to suggest criteria for determining those elements which are to be included in the description of a value system, and those elements which are to be excluded; and (c) to indicate a method of description that is, in part, numerical.

Second, some consideration will be given to the development of related micro-theoretical concepts, and third, an attempt will be made to show the connection between these micro-theoretical concepts and the macro-theoretical concepts discussed heretofore.

Toward the Definition of a Value System[3]

A value system may affect such disparate phenomena as: (1) the average age at marriage, (2) the desire to have children, (3) the spacing of births, (4) the use of contraceptive devices, (5) the attitude toward abortion, (6) attitudes toward infanticide, (7) coital frequency, (8) the extent of extra-marital sexual relations, (9) diet, (10) cleanliness and hygiene, (11) family solidarity and attitudes toward migration, etc. It is clear that all of the activites mentioned above, and others that could be mentioned, will affect the size, growth, and composition of the population through their effects on fertility, mortality, and migration. To the extent that values affect these activities they affect population change. And if we could describe our system of values in such a way as to indicate the extent to which they affect the system of human choices implied by such activities then we would have some notion of the effect of a value system on population growth.

In order to avoid confusion a distinction should be made between values that affect the choice of means and values that reflect or are concerned with the determination of ends. An appreciation of

---

[3] At this point a slight hedge is in order. What follows may be somewhat different than the notion of a value system held by some sociologists or social pscychologists. If so, this should not be looked upon as an attempt to produce a superior model. No claim for the utility of the concepts is made beyond the scope of the subject matter considered here.

this distinction is vital if the reader is to get a correct view of what follows. In this essay we shall be concerned solely with values that affect the choice of means.

The word "value" suggests that a value system is somehow related to a process of individual or social valuation; or to propositions which reflect such valuations. This being so, it is desirable to distinguish between the kind of propositions which can conceivably reflect such valuations and the kind which cannot.

A basic distinction is to be made between normative and non-normative propositions; or between propositions in the imperative mood and those in the indicative mood. Talcott Parsons[4] distinguishes between normative propositions and experiential propositions; that is, between propositions that suggest obligation, duty, or desired standard of behavior and propositions that are factual or conceivably factual.

Still another way of putting it is that we distinguish between "ought" propositions and "is" propositions. With respect to "ought" propositions we have in mind only those propositions where the verb "ought" implies a moral imperative, or a moral injunctive, and not those where the verb implies expectation of some sort. For example, we are not concerned with such propositions as "You ought to be good at this," or "You ought to like that." Now, an "ought" proposition, or what we shall hereafter call a normative proposition, need not have the verb "ought" as the major verb; we include in our category of normative propositions any proposition that can be translated into an equivalent proposition where the major verb is "ought."

We can conceive of the possibility of representing values by normative propositions -- propositions in the imperative mood containing an injunction or imperative of some sort. Such propositions would indicate what a certain individual or a given set of individuals believe ought to or ought not to be done under a given set of circumstances. Also, for a given set of alternatives, imperatives can be translated into injunctions by prohibiting the choice of all but one of the alternatives. Hence there is no loss in generality in describing

---

[4] The Structure of Social Action. New York: McGraw-Hill, 1937, pp. 74 ff.

a set of values only in terms of injunctions (e.g. "Thou shalt not kill ....") rather than both imperatives and injunctions. Tentatively, we can define a value system as a set of normative propositions that indicate the prohibitions recognized by some or all members of a society as limiting the behavior of these members in some degree.

Basic Propositions and Summary Propositions

Normative propositions may be on various levels of abstraction. It is often possible to state two normative propositions so that one of these is a special case of the other. The question a- rises whether in a case of this kind both propositions belong to a description of the same system of values, or whether the inclusion of both clutters up the description with unnecessary propositions. It is certainly clear that normative propositions may be of various degrees of specificity, and that it is therefore desirable to distinguish between propositions on the lowest level of specificity necessary for the pur- poses at hand, and those not on that level. We will therefore dis- tinguish between summary propositions and basic propositions. A summary proposition is one that can be reduced to two or more spe- cific normative propositions for the purposes at hand. A basic propo- sition is one that is on the lowest level of abstraction desirable for the problem under consideration. That is, a basic proposition is one which it is not profitable or possible to reduce to two or more specific norma- tive propositions. We should note that in many cases it may be possible to reduce a normative proposition to a number of equivalent more spe- cific propositions, but that for the purposes of handling a certain prob- lem it may not be profitable or desirable to do so. Thus, what may be a summary proposition in one case may be a basic proposition in an- other. Now, given these definitions it follows that from a value sys- tem enumerating completely all the basic and summary propositions belonging to it, we can remove all the summary propositions without reducing the content of the system. We could call such a set of basic propositions the elements of the value system; and we could call any basic proposition belonging to the set an element of the value system.

The Reduction Problem

Part of the notion being developed here is based on the assumption that the recognition of values is possible. That is, we be- gin with the assumption that individuals have the ability to recognize

and indicate whether or not they follow the injunction implied in a certain normative proposition. For example, if we ask an individual
whether he believes that he adheres to the injunction implied in the
proposition: "Thou shalt not kill, except in self defense," it is likely
that he would be able to come forth with a definite yes or no. In other
cases it may be necessary to add more qualifications to the proposition
before the person felt that he could answer it definitely. In any case,
we are probably not making an heroic assumption when we assume
that an investigator can elicit replies to questions of this sort that
will indicate whether an individual believes he adheres or does not
adhere to any or all of the injunctions implied in a set of normative
propositions. Submitting an individual to a questioning process of
this kind would reveal the value system of the individual.

If an individual were asked whether he would adhere to
the norm implied in the proposition "Thou shalt not kill," he may reply that he generally would but that there would be circumstances
where he would not, such as, in time of war in his capacity as a
soldier, or in self defense, or in order to protect his family and
home, etc. However, if the proposition "Thou shalt not kill," were reduced to a number of propositions beginning with "Thou shalt not
kill," and ending with the description of a circumstance under which
the prohibition against killing was to hold, it is likely that the subject
would be able to reply with a definite yes or no answer as to whether
he adheres to the injunction implied in each proposition. Should there
be a case where the subject could not reply with a definite yes or no
answer then the normative proposition could be broken up into two or
more such propositions where the circumstances were spelled out in
a more specific manner. If such a process of the reduction of abstract propositions to more specific propositions were to go on long
enough then it seems that a point must be reached in which the circumstances in every normative proposition are made specific enough
so that a yes or no reply can be given. Because of the possibility of
reducing abstract normative propositions to propositions of a more
specific nature it appears that the possible multi-valued reaction to a
normative proposition is not a real problem. Thus, in any description
of a value system it is necessary that the normative propositions be
reduced to a level of specificity so that adherence or lack of adherence

to the proposition can be clearly determined.

Every normative proposition can be divided into two
parts. The first part will be of an imperative or injunctive nature,
and the second will give the circumstance or circumstances under
which the imperative or injunction is to apply. (In some cases the
circumstances may not be stated in the proposition. If communicability exists then the circumstances are understood. If the circumstances are not implied or understood in some way or other then the
proposition is meaningless.) For example, in the proposition:
"Soldiers should obey their officers when on duty," the first part,
"Soldiers should obey their officers," indicates the imperative, while
the second part, "when on duty," indicates the circumstances under
which the imperative is to hold. The phrase "when on duty" is of an
abstract nature, and it can be reduced to a number of phrases each
one of which indicates a more specific kind of duty. If for the first
part of a normative proposition we write the symbol N, and if for
each circumstance under which the injunction or imperative can conceivably apply we write C, then if there are n circumstances we
can write the summary proposition as

$$N(C_1 \text{ v } C_2 \text{ v } ... \text{ v } C_n),$$

where v stands for the word "or" as sometimes used in symbolic
logic. Each of the n basic propositions that are equivalent to the
summary proposition can then be written NC_1, NC_2, ..., NC_n. If
for every proposition NC_i an individual can give an affirmative
(= 1) or a negative (= 0) reply to indicate adherence or lack of adherence to the norm, then these propositions may be considered as
elements of the value system.[5] If an individual cannot give an affirmative or negative reply to a proposition NC_i, then this proposition
is itself a summary proposition, and it should be broken up into two
or more propositions where the circumstances in each proposition
are indicated with a greater degree of specificity. This gives us our

[5] Because of lack of possible symbols, some of the symbols used in
previous chapters are being used again with different meanings attached. Thus, the C's have a different meaning than the C's in previous
previous chapters.

rule for determining the degree of specificity to which a summary
proposition should be reduced in order to determine the elements of
the value system. Any question about adherence to a normative proposition which can be answered definitely by a positive or negative reply by all of those being questioned need not be made more specific.
Any proposition where the reply is indefinite (e.g. "it depends," "perhaps," "yes and no," etc.) should be reduced to propositions of a greater degree of specificity.

   If adequate communicability between investigator and
subject exists then the relationship between the response to summary
propositions and the equivalent basic propositions is clear. If the
response to the summary proposition $N(C_1 \vee C_2 \vee \ldots \vee C_n)$ is indefinite (yes and no) then the response to at least two of the basic
propositions, say NC_i and NC_j must be different; that is, the response to one proposition will be positive and the other negative. If
the response to the summary proposition is positive, then the response to all the basic propositions must be positive. Similarly, if
the response to the summary proposition is negative, then the response to all the basic propositions must be negative. If the response
to one of a number of basic propositions is different from the rest,
then the response to the summary proposition must be indefinite.

   Most summary normative propositions we come across
in every day discourse or reading are incompletely stated summary
propositions. That is, they do not list all of the conceivable alternate
circumstances under which the injunction or imperative is to apply.
Symbolically, they do not include all of the $\vee C$'s in the statement of
the summary proposition that belong to the summary proposition.
In a specific investigation this may lead to apparent inconsistencies
(e.g. a positive response to the summary proposition and a negative
response to one or more of the basic propositions) which may merely indicate inadequate communicability between investigator and subject. That is, the subject had in mind or inferred a different set of
$\vee C$'s from the incompletely stated summary proposition than the investigator had in mind.

The Value System and the Field of Action

   We are interested in values not for their own sake but
only to the extent that they affect human decisions and human behavior.

It is therefore desirable to relate normative propositions that reflect
values to such decisions. In order to do so it may help if we look upon
a value system as a set of ethical "rules" that affect behavior. We
look upon every element of a value system as a rule. As rules, the
elements of a value system in some way govern a "field of action,"
or a set of alternatives. Now, rules are meaningless apart from the
fields of action that they govern. For example, the rules of chess are
meaningless apart from the game of chess. A rule in some way limits
or directs the choice between alternatives. This is really two sides
of the same coin. A rule that directs the choice of A among alternatives A, B, and C, essentially limits the choice to A since it
prohibits the choosing of either B or C. However, a rule need not
direct the choice, it may merely limit the range of choice. Thus, if
the alternatives are A, B, and C the rule may prohibit the choice
of C and limit the choice to A or B. The essence of rules, then,
is that they limit free choice. Where choice is absent rules are
otiose. Where the rule does not limit choice it is meaningless. Thus,
given a field of action, an element of a value system may be conceived as a rule that limits the effective field of action; that is,
something that limits the range of alternatives.

Since the meaningfulness of an element of a value sys-
tem depends on its relationship to a field of action it is desirable to
indicate exactly what is meant by a field of action. First, let us consider the notion of a "situation." A "situation" may be conceived as
a concrete circumstance in which a choice between alternatives has
to be made, and where choosing one alternative eliminates the possibility of choosing any other alternative. We may now conceive a field
of action as the set of "situations" where the alternatives are of the
same kind. We can now view an element of a value system as something that prohibits the choice of an alternative within a given field of
action.[6]

---

[6] We may note that the system of action described here differs somewhat from the system of action outlined by Parsons in The Structure
of Social Action (op. cit.). In Parsons' system the unit act is the
primordial element of the construct, while in the construct outlined
above an alternative (a choice), within a group of alternatives (a field
of action) to achieve a certain end, is our primordial element.

Values and Performance

It may be argued that the verbalized value system may
not really be effective. That is, people may say that certain normative propositions reflect their values although their behavior would
indicate otherwise. However, the possibility of this condition existing need not change our conception of an element of a value system.
It means merely that we have to distinguish between the verbalized
value system whose elements would limit the field of action if they
were adhered to, and what may be called the "effective value system"
whose elements actually limit the fields of action as indicated by observed behavior. This implies, essentially, that to give a full description of a value system it may be necessary to obtain three kinds
of information. These are: (1) the beliefs of each individual about
his own adherence to each element of the system; (2) the beliefs of
each individual about the general acceptability by the society as a
whole of each element of the system; and (3) the actual adherence by
each individual to each element of the system as indicated by his
behavior.

Now we cannot enter into the inner recesses of the
mind of every member of a population and determine whether he adheres to the values he says he adheres to, or whether he is hypocritical with respect to some of the values. All that we can do at this
point is to indicate the type of information that would have to be a-
vailable in order to determine whether a verbalized value is effective
or not.

Given any situation in which a choice has to be made
one of the conceivable alternatives may be the one that an "ethical
rule" or value prohibits. If this choice is the choice that would have
been made in the absence of the "ethical rule" but is not made, then
we could say that that element in the value system is effective for the
field of action of which that situation is a member. It is obvious, however, that an alternative may be avoided for reasons other than the
operation of an "ethical rule." Only when the alternative is the one
that would have been chosen apart from the effectiveness of the element of the value system in question can the effectiveness of the value
be tested. It follows that in order to determine the effectiveness of
a value through observation it is necessary to know the rule of

selection between alternatives. Where the value system is the rule of
selection between alternatives it may be possible to tell adherence to
the value system as such but not to any individual element in the system. In order to have conclusive evidence of adherence it would be
necessary to have some evidence that the value chosen would not have
been chosen anyhow. Whether such evidence can be obtained in any
specific case will depend on the amount of knowledge and the state of
development of the various sciences that are and can be brought to
bear on the specific situation. This, however, is an empirical question.
For purposes of creating a theoretical construct that is logically consistent it is only necessary to specify clearly the elements that enter
into the theory. The question of application is a different matter. It
is not unusual for theories to ask for more than they can get and still
be of some use.

The Value System and the Rule of Selection

There is no reason why in any system there should be
only one rule of selection between alternatives. It may very well be
that for every field of action there is a different rule of selection.
Now, the point to be made here is that the value system cannot be considered apart from the rule of selection with respect to any field of
action if the value system is effective. In those cases where the value
system limits all of the alternatives but one, and the values are adhered to, then the value system is clearly the rule of selection. In
those cases where the value system does not exhaust all of the alternatives but one, the choice has to be made on the basis of additional
criteria. Here, the elements of the value system pertaining to the
particular field of action, plus the additional criteria used, form the
rule of selection. There may be cases where the criteria for choosing
between alternatives and the elements of the value system overlap;
that is, the criterion for selection might dictate a choice which an
element of the value system prohibits. In such a case the question of
dominance enters the picture. If the elements of the value system are
really effective, that is if they dominate any other criteria for selection, then any other criteria for selection are operative only with respect to those alternatives not prohibited by the elements of the value
system. Here again, the value system plus the additional criteria
form the rule of selection. By way of summary we may say that a rule

of selection is a statement of the procedure for choosing between alternatives, and that the independent effective elements of the value
system pertaining to the set of alternatives in question is part of the
statement of such a procedure.

The Description of a Value System

For purposes of determining behavior the basic norma-
tive propositions are important only in that they reflect values which,
if adhered to, prohibit the choice of one or more alternatives in a
given field of action. It would therefore appear to be reasonable to
equate the normative propositions reflecting values to the alternatives
that they prohibit. We begin with a set of n alternatives of a field of
action F. Each value can be represented by the alternative that it
prohibits if adhered to.

Now, by a response we mean an indication of adherence
or lack of adherence to the injunction in a given normative proposition.
Thus, responses are two-valued. They either indicate adherence
(= 1) or lack of adherence (= 0) to the normative proposition in
question.

For a fairly complete picture of the operation of a set
of values in a society it may be necessary to specify the following
five types of information about each value.

(a) The individual verbalized value system. Let $\hat{a}_{ij}$[7]
represent the response to the ith value by the jth individual. Set
$\hat{a}_{ij} = 1$ if the jth individual claims that he adheres to the ith value.
Set $\hat{a}_{ij} = 0$ if the jth individual claims that he does not adhere to the
i^{th} value. If there are m individuals then

$$\alpha_i = \frac{\sum_j \hat{a}_{ij}}{m}$$

represents the proportion of the population that claims adherence to
the ith value.

---

[7] The symbols marked with a circumflex should not be confused with
similar symbols without the circumflex which were used in previous
chapters. Lack of sufficient letters in the English alphabet forced the
used of this device.

(b) <u>The societal value system</u>. Set $\hat{b}_{ij} = 1$ if the jth individual believes that the community at large generally adheres to the ith value. Set $\hat{b}_{ij} = 0$ if the jth individual does not so believe. In this case we let

$$\beta_i = \frac{\sum\limits_{j} \hat{b}_{ij}}{m}$$

represent the proportion of the population that believes that the ith value is generally adhered to.

(c) <u>Actual adherence to the value system</u>. Similarly, set $\hat{c}_{ij} = 1$ if in actual situations the jth individual adheres to the ith value, and set $\hat{c}_{ij} = 0$ if he does not.

$$\gamma_i = \frac{\sum\limits_{j} \hat{c}_{ij}}{m}$$

represents the proportion of the population that actually adheres to value i.

(d) Set $\hat{b}'_{ij} = 1$ if the jth individual believes that the community at large adheres to the ith value, and if he also claims adherence to the ith value, otherwise set $\hat{b}'_{ij} = 0$. Then

$$\beta'_i = \frac{\sum\limits_{j} \hat{b}'_{ij}}{\sum\limits_{j} \hat{b}_{ij}}$$

represents the proportion of those who gave a positive response in (b) who also gave a positive response in (a).

(e) Similarly, set $\hat{c}'_{ij} = 1$ if the jth individual believes that the community at large adheres to the ith value, if he claims adherence to the ith value, and if in actual practice he adheres to the ith value. Then

$$\gamma'_i = \frac{\sum\limits_{j} \hat{c}'_{ij}}{\sum\limits_{j} \hat{b}'_{ij}}$$

represents the proportion of those who responded positively in (d) and who also gave a positive response in (c).

For most purposes the effect of the ith value on the behavior of the society with respect to field of action F would be ade-
quately described by α_i, β_i, γ_i, β_i', and γ_i'. Similarly, the effect of the
value system on the entire field of action can be adequately described
by a table of five columns and n rows, if there are n alternatives in
the field of action. The typical row, say the ith row, would contain the
proportions α_i, β_i, γ_i, β_i' , and γ_i' . From such a setup we can also
obtain some derived indices that may be of interest for some purposes.
For example, β_i β_i' may be looked upon as an index of verbalized
conformity to the societal value in question if β_i is large. If β_i
is small then we may seriously question whether the prohibition representing the ith value is recognized by the population at large.
Similarly, β_i β_i' γ_i' may be looked upon as an index of the effectiveness of the societal value in question, again if β_i is relatively large.
Thus, estimates of α_i, β_i, γ_i, β_i', γ_i', and any related indices that
could be concocted, would give an investigator some idea of how sig-
nificant a given set of values was in affecting the behavior of a population facing the alternatives that make up the field of action under
consideration.

The Representation of Values in Theoretical Models

The requirements for an adequate description of a value system suggested in the previous section are more demanding than
is necessary for the kind of models to be considered. For most purposes all the knowledge necessary is the extent of actual adherence
to the system of values. Thus, for the ith alternative in the field of
action it may be sufficient to know the value of γ_i. We shall see that
a more convenient form of representation is to use $1 - \gamma_i = V_i$, for
all i. In this case V_i indicates the proportion of the population that
is free to choose the ith alternative if it wishes; more correctly, it
is the proportion of the population whose virtual (but not necessarily
actual, since some other alternative may be chosen) choice of alternative i is unencumbered by adherence to a value that would prohibit
such a choice. $V_i = 1$ indicates that every member of the population
facing that field of action is free to choose the ith alternative. On the
other hand, $V_i = 0$ indicates that regardless of the other criteria for
choice the ith alternative would not be chosen. Obviously V_i cannot
be greater than one or less than zero. If $V_i = .3$, it indicates that

30% of the population are free to choose the ith alternative, although they may not do so on other grounds.

In any real situation it may be exceedingly difficult to get an accurate picture of the magnitude of γ_i, for any i. In that case α_i may have to be employed as a substitute for γ_i. The important question, in such an eventuality, is to what extent is α_i, or a figure derived from α_i, a reasonable estimate of the unknown γ_i. Here, a knowledge of some of the other aspects of the value system may be useful in appraising the substitutability of α for γ. For example, it may be found that in other cases where the magnitude of some γ is ascertainable, there is a correlation between the magnitudes of α, β, and γ. It is conceivable that when the magnitudes of α and β are close together then the magnitudes of α and γ are close together and that when α and β are far apart then so are α and γ. That is people may know how their neighbors really behave and this would be reflected in the relative magnitudes of α, β, and γ. The main point here is simply this: Although the magnitudes of α, β, γ, β', and γ', need not all be used in the description of a value system, the magnitudes that are not employed directly in the model may be necessary indirectly in assessing the probable accuracy of the estimates that are employed.

Consideration of a few polar cases may be of interest: Suppose that $\alpha_i = 1$, $\beta_i = 1$, $\gamma'_i = 0$. This reflects a situation in which the value in question has no real effectiveness with respect to behavior. While the entire population pays lip service to the ith value they are hypocritical in their behavior. But this case reflects a highly unstable situation. Unless everyone remains completely ignorant of everyone else's sentiments and behavior on the question, the magnitude of β_i is bound to decline. As the value of β_i approaches zero there would be less and less reason for people to claim that they adhere to the ith value when in fact they do not. It would appear from this that in the absence of ignorance, or with regular channels of overcoming ignorance, the magnitudes of α_i, β_i, and γ_i would have to be pretty close together for the situation to be in stable equilibrium. It would be easy to concoct examples of other unstable cases which would generally be characterized by considerable divergence between α_i, β_i, and γ_i. The efficiency of the organized and unorganized means of communication and dissemination of information determines, in part, the maximum divergence between α_i, β_i, and γ_i, that is consistent with stability.

At this point it may be in order to consider some serious objections that may conceivably be raised to much of the above discussion. It may be argued, for example, that underlying the above schema is the implicit assumption that human behavior is always purposive, and further it may be argued that the above model assumes that people always know the principles and values upon which they make decisions, or upon which they will make decisions at some future time. It may be indicated that such underlying assumptions are invalid since numerous counter examples can be found in which the assumptions do not hold. Values may not always be given. There are real conflicts of conscience or principle. People do sometimes sincerely believe that they will behave in accordance with one set of principles but when placed in an actual situation behave otherwise. An individual may often be unable to visualize how he will behave in a certain situation until he is actually placed in it, and so on.

In reply to all this it may be well to repeat the statement made at the very beginning of the chapter: viz., that no claim is made for the utility of this model beyond those aspects of behavior pertinent to demographic or economic theories. Implicit in such a statement is the qualification that there may be numerous types of behavior to which the above model could not be applied. Whether all human behavior is purposive or not may depend on the definition of purposive. If purposive behavior implies doing something to achieve a given end that the individual has in mind, then the above model does not necessarily assume purposive behavior. The model implies only that individuals face periodically certain definite alternatives, one of which may be the alternative of not doing anything.

Of course, it must be granted that there may be certain types of behavior, such as explorative behavior, where the above model may not apply, since an individual may not really be able to know whether or not he will adhere to a certain value in an untried and unknown situation. It is submitted, however, that the type of behavior significant in demographic-economic models is, for the most part, repetitive and known. That is to say, the situations which demographic-

economic theory assumes an individual to face are usually well defined and of a type that is probably faced over and over again.
Finally, it may be pointed out that the above model is not presented
as something rigid and determined for all time, but only as a first
step toward the development of superior models.

Values, Rules of Selection and Choice Distributions

The effect of the value system on choice is best des-
cribed by the γ column if the data are available, and if not, then the
α column, or an adjusted α column, is probably the best estimate of
the γ column. It will be recalled that we set $V_i = 1 - \gamma_i$ (or one
minus the best estimate of γ_i), for all i, as a convenient way of
representing the set of values (pertaining to a given field of action)
in static models. V_i represents the proportion of those confronting
the field of action who have no aversion to choosing the ith alternative because of the operation of the value system, although they may
not necessarily choose that alternative for some other reason. It
follows that if for any field of action

$$\sum_{i=1}^{n} V_i = 1$$

where $1, 2, ..., i, ..., n$ are the alternatives, then the value system
is the rule of selection, if the values are independent and non-
competing.

At this point it is convenient to introduce the notion of
a choice distribution. A choice distribution indicates the proportions
of those confronting a given field of action who choose the various
alternatives. The sum of the proportions must obviously be equal to
unity since, by definition, a person cannot choose more than one alternative simultaneously. Let d_i stand for the proportion that chose
the ith alternative in field of action F; $d_1 + d_2 ... + d_i ... + d_n = 1$.
Now, the choice distribution is an ex-post datum. It can only be ascertained after the event; that is, it is the end result of the decision-
making process. For purposes of prediction we are interested in the
factors that determine the choice distribution. Given these notions
it is clear that the rule of selection plus the necessary parameters
determine the choice distribution for a given field of action. If the

V's for a given field of action equal the corresponding elements of the choice distribution for that field of action then the column V completely defines the rule of selection. This is the case only where

$$\sum_{i=1}^{n} V_i = \sum_{i=1}^{n} d_i = 1,$$

where the values are independent and non-competing. Of course,

$$\sum_{i=1}^{n} V_i$$

can be greater than

$$\sum_{i=1}^{n} d_i ,$$

in which case the rule of selection is not completely defined by the value system. This suggests a criterion for the definition of the rule of selection. We can say that the rule of selection is defined when, given the parameters that effect choice, the rule of selection so defined completely determines the choice distribution of the field of action being considered.

Now, according to our criterion, if

$$\sum_{i=1}^{n} V_i > 1$$

then the value system by itself does not give us a fully defined rule of selection; that is, the value system will prohibit the choice of less than. n - 1 alternatives for some or all individuals. From the alternatives not prohibited a choice will have to be made on the basis of some other criteria or "sub rules" of selection which, of course, should be specified in any particular model.

Role and Role Structure

A few more concepts are needed before we can tie the various ideas into a neat bundle. First, consider the concepts of role and role structure. We define a role as a set of fields of action confronting an individual plus the specification of the frequency that each

field of action in the set confronts an individual during a unit period.[8]
For clarification, the following are examples of the definition of specific roles, S_1, S_2 and S_3: $S_1 = F_1$, $S_2 = F_2 + 2F_3$, $S_3 = 2F_2 + 3F_3 +$
$5F_4$. In the example, an individual in role S_2 would face field of
action F_2 once and field of action F_3 twice during the unit period.
The other two roles would be interpreted in a similar manner. For
convenience, in any specific model, it would probably be best to choose
a unit period sufficiently short so that the frequencies with which the
fields of action confront an individual in a given role are the smallest
integers possible. However, the choice of a period too short may lead
to contradiction with the definition of a field of action since it is impossible to be confronted by a fraction of a field of action.

By role structure we refer to the number of the popula-
tion in each of the roles considered. Thus, $s_1 S_1$, $s_2 S_2$, ..., $s_i S_i$, ...,
$s_n S_n$ would be a statement of a given role structure where S_i is
the ith role and s_i is the number of individuals in that role.

$$\sum_{i=1}^{n} s_i$$

can be greater than the total population since some individuals can be
in more than one role. Occupational distributions are examples of
role structures -- although, in this case, the roles are usually not defined in such a way as to be directly related with the individual decision-making process.

The Aggregate Consequences of a Choice Distribution

The reason we are concerned with rules of selection,
fields of action, and choice distributions is that we believe different
rules of selection and their resulting choice distributions yield different consequences which are of interest. That is, every choice distribution will yield a given set of consequences of an economic, demographic

---

[8] Professor W. E. Moore has indicated that what I have defined as
role some sociologists have called status. I persist in using the term
role because it comes closer to the non-sociologist's concept of the
notion. Facing a certain field of action implies playing a part which in
turn implies the concept of being in a certain role. Cf. Ralph Linton,
The Study of Man. New York: D. Appleton-Century Company, 1936,
Chapter VIII, "Status and Role," pp. 113 ff.

or sociological nature, depending on the fields of action being considered. For example, the choice distribution of a given set of entrepreneurs in a given industry may result in a certain output of the product
at a certain price. In this case the specific output and price of the
commodity may be conceived as the aggregate consequences of the
choice distribution in question. If the consequences of choosing certain alternatives are independent of each other then the aggregate consequences of a choice distribution are simply the sum of the consequences of choosing each particular alternative, where the consequences
of a particular choice are a function of the number choosing that alternative. The consequences of a certain portion of the population
choosing a certain alternative may depend on what proportions of the
population choose the remaining alternatives, in which case the problem is more complex and the outcome will depend on the functional
relationships between the consequences of a certain proportion choosing a certain alternative and what other proportions choose other alternatives.

       Now, it is possible that the consequences of choosing
certain alternatives cannot be put in quantitative terms, but we limit
our investigation to those fields of action where the consequences of
the alternatives can be conceived in such terms. If quantitative, the
consequences of certain alternatives may be a specific amount or they
may be a probability distribution, depending on the nature of the field
of action being considered. For example, in economics, the output of
a certain product for a firm, which is the consequence of the entre-
preneur choosing certain alternatives, will be a specific determinate
amount, while in demography the consequences, say, of using a certain contraceptive method cannot be determined uniquely but may be
described in terms of a probability distribution. The point in all of
this is simply the notion that a choice distribution has consequences
and, therefore, a given choice distribution plus the functional relationships between the choice distribution and the relevant parameters implies a set of consequences of an economic or demographic nature that
can be stated in quantitative terms.

       <u>Relationship</u> <u>between</u> <u>Concepts</u> <u>Considered</u> <u>Heretofore</u>

       In this section an attempt will be made to relate the
various concepts introduced thus far. They can all be integrated into

a rather simple chain of reasoning.

We begin with the role structure as a datum. This gives the number in each role during the unit period. Given the definition of each role we can determine the total number of times each field of action confronts someone in the population. (For each field of action this total is the sum of the products of the frequency with which the field of action comes up in each role and the number of people in that role.) This implies a knowledge of the number of times the same set of alternatives confronts someone during the unit period since each field of action is defined in terms of a specific set of alternatives. If the complete definition of the rule of selection (of which the value system is a part) is known then we can determine what the choice distribution for the pertinent field of action will be when the rule of selection operates on that field of action in each and every case. That is, we can determine the number of times each alternative is picked by the population as a whole. In a similar manner we can do the same thing for every field of action in the model. Since each alternative implies a consequence of some sort the determination of the choice distribution permits in turn the estimation of the aggregate consequences of the operation of the model. In any specific demographic-economic model of this sort the end result of such a procedure would be a set of demographic and/or economic consequences (e.g. the number of births, the number of marriages, the amount of production, the value of the national income, the standard of living, etc.) for the unit period. Models of this sort are probably not of interest in themselves, partly because of the high degree of oversimplification involved, and partly because they are limited to one period, but their value may lie in forming the basis of more complicated models that handle relationships between periods.

II

We are now at a point where we have to consider the problem of integrating the concepts developed in this chapter with the aggregative models. That is to say, we have to consider the possibility of constructing "sub-models" which explain the determination of the major variables period by period. For present purposes it is probably sufficient to concentrate our attention on the determination of the magnitudes of those variables that were most significant in our discussions of the aggregative and multi-sector models (i.e., on the A's, a's, r's, and R's). However, no attempt will be made to work out completely detailed models based on specific rules of selection, fields of action, and/or the nature of the economy in concrete instances. Among the reasons for not attempting to do so is that too many sets of alternative assumptions are both possible and reasonable. All that will be done is to outline the way in which detailed sub-models can conceivably be constructed if all of the requisite empirical information were available.

In most models certain information or data are assumed to be available, obtainable, or given at the outset. In this discussion the necessary data assumed to be given, or obtained in some manner or other, are of the following three kinds.

(1) The occupational role structure. We conceive of the population divided into a number of roles, with some individuals in more than one role. The individuals in some roles will choose between entering or not entering some occupation, in others they will choose between remaining in their present occupation or shifting to another one, and in still others they will choose between remaining in the labor force or retiring. In still other roles we are interested in the individuals have the choice between saving and not saving, and between investing in one kind of investment good rather than another. The roles are defined by the fields of action the individuals face, plus the number of times a specific field of action is faced in any given period. Where government officials make decisions with respect to investment they too are to be included within the occupational role structure.

(2) The fields of action. The pertinent fields of action can be divided into two categories. In the first category are those fields of action which have to do with the determination of the size and nature of the investment for the period; the second category includes those fields of action which have to do with the size and distribution of the working labor force. In the first category the fields of action would specify the investment alternatives open to each group facing the same set of investment opportunities. Since some investment opportunities are likely to be open to some individuals but not to others we would expect quite a number of separate fields of action in the first category.

The fields of action in the second category would indicate the specific
alternatives open to individuals, in each role, to enter the labor force
or not, to shift from their present occupation to some other occupation,
or to leave the labor force. In many cases the actual choice would depend on the employment opportunities available, and hence included
among the fields of action in the second category should be fields of action that specify the alternatives open to employers to hire or not to
hire a certain number of other individuals.

        (3) The rules of selection. For every field of action
there must be a rule of selection of some sort. It is conceivable, of
course, that a given rule of selection should be applicable to more
than one field of action. The same rule of selection may even apply
to all of the fields of action in the same category. Indeed, this may be
a useful assumption to make as a first approximation. (As a matter
of fact this is precisely what is done in micro-economic theory.) But
this need not be the case. Not only may there be separate rules of
selection for those facing different fields of action but there may be
different rules of selection employed by different individuals facing
the same field of action. In any case the rules of selection employed
by the individuals in each role must be obtained. The rules of selection are central to models of this kind, for without them it would be
impossible to determine the choices that are made during the period,
and hence without them it would be impossible to infer the outcome of
events for the period. Of course, what the rules of selection really
are in concrete cases is an empirical matter.

        For the fields of action in the first category the rules
of selection would have to explain how the specific choices are made
for every set of alternative investment opportunities. One possibility
is that the rule of selection for fields of action of this sort can be a
profit maximization principle of some sort. But other rules of selection are conceivable. This is especially likely to be the case for the
type of investments governments may engage in. Values also enter the
picture. For example, we would not expect devout Hindus to invest
and engage in cattle slaughtering enterprises, even if this should happen
to be the most profitable investment opportunity available.

        For the fields of action in the second category the rules
of selection would have to explain how some chose to enter the labor

force while others chose to leave, and on what basis some chose to
leave, and on what basis some chose to shift from one occupation to
another while others did not. For example, it is an empirical observation that in a developing economy certain shifts in the labor
force take place as average income rises. Usually the proportion in
so-called primary industries declines, while the proportion in secondary industries increases up to a point, but the proportion in tertiary
industries apparently continues to increase as average income increases.[9] The rules of selection applicable to the fields of action in
the second category should be able to explain, in part, this phenomenon, in those circumstances where it takes place.

From the occupational role structure, the fields of ac-
tion, and the rules of selection we should be able to infer certain things
about the outcome of events during the period. First, the operation of
the rules of selection on the pertinent fields of action, plus the number
facing each field of action, determines the choice distributions; i.e.
the proportion and number of those facing a given field of action that
choose each alternative. For the fields of action in the first category
the rules of selection would determine the quantities and types of investment for the period.

The operation of the rules of selection on the fields of
action in the second category should determine all of the shifts in the
occupational structure other than those due to death. This information plus the death rates for each occupational grouping should yield
the occupational role distribution that we begin with in the next period.
(Of course, the births of a number of previous periods must, indirectly, also be taken into account since, in part, they determine the
numbers in successive groups that are just about to enter the labor
force.) We thus have one set of data or initial information for the

---

[9] On this point see the following: Louis H. Bean, "International Industrialization and Per Capita Income," Part V, pp. 119-144 in:
Conference on Research in Income and Wealth, Studies in Income and
Wealth, Vol. 8. New York: National Bureau of Economic Research,
1946; Colin Clark, Conditions of Economic Progress. London: Macmillan Co., 1940, Chapter 5; Roy Glenday, "Long-Period Economic
Trends," Journal of the Royal Statistical Society, Vol. 101, No. 3 (1938),
pp. 511-552. See also P. T. Bauer and B. S. Yamey, "Economic Progress
and Occupational Distribution," Economic Journal, Vol. 61, No. 244
(Dec., 1951), pp. 741-755, for a dissenting opinion on this question.

next period.

Now, if we redefine our notion of a sector in a special way, that is, as a set of roles, then the foregoing yields a method of relating some of the elements of micro-economic behavior to the central variables of the multi-sector models.

The investment and occupational opportunities open in the second period depend, in part, on the investment alternatives chosen in the first period and, in part, on such exogenous factors as innovations, changes in the terms of trade, changes in exchange rates, etc. One way in which investment in one period determines and stimulates investment in the next period is through complementarities in production, or what may be called production links.[10] Consider the case of investment in a completely new industry -- one that was not hitherto represented in the productive structure of the economy. Some industries require other industries to service them, to process raw materials to a stage at which the second industry takes them up, to build, repair, replace, and maintain the capital goods of the new industry, to supply specialized or professional services of one kind or another, etc. In view of these links between industries, investment in a new industry will stimulate expansion in existing industries, or stimulate the introduction of other new industries, or, most likely, stimulate both simultaneously. Changes in the methods of production of already produced products may also stimulate the introduction of new industries, but the investment in existing industries where the productive processes are not changed probably stimulates only the expansion of other existing industries. Thus, investment in one period may open up similar or different investment opportunities in the next, depending on the nature of investment in the first, and on the production links involved. In the early stages of economic development when many new industries are being introduced the stimulus to investment in other new industries is probably greatest, and the magnitude of the B's probably highest. The marginal efficiency of capital in a new industry is likely to be high in the early stages of the development of

---

[10] One of the great gaps in the existing economic literature is an acceptable theory of capital accumulation or capital growth. For an excellent summary and evaluation of the existing theories see Paul H. Douglas, The Theory of Wages. New York: The Macmillan Company, 1934, Chapters 17 and 18.

that industry since the advantages of scale are gradually being
achieved, and diminishing returns due to crowding on the less elastic
factors are less likely to set in in the early stages. Eventually a point
will be reached where the stimulus to new industries will be very much
lower for a number of reasons. First, as more and more industries
are being introduced it becomes easier to meet the needs of additional new industries through the expansion of the existing ones and,
second, it may be found that it becomes more difficult or uneconomical
to introduce additional complementary industries either due to lack of
requisite natural resources, or because it becomes less expensive to
obtain the complementary goods through international trade even after
transportation costs are added. The older industries are more likely
to be beyond the points of optimum size than the new ones, and hence
greater investment in existing industries in the later stages of economic development is likely to lead to lower values of B, i.e. of the
income-capital ratio. However, inventions and innovations that may
occur during such a period of change may alter existing trends in the
magnitudes of B for a time. Much of the above discussion has been
couched in terms of likelihood and probability for it is recognized that
in the last analysis these are really empirical matters.

Also, investment in one period determines, in part, the
employment opportunities open in the next period, and hence the fields
of action in the second category are determined for successive periods.

The Population Growth Function -- Outline of a
Sub-model

The conclusions reached in previous chapters depend
to a considerable extent on the nature of the population growth function
that is postulated. We saw that in some cases a population growth
function in which the rate of growth was a monotonic increasing function of average income led to one conclusion, while a population growth
function in which the rate of population growth was a monotonic decreasing function for levels of average income beyond a certain point
led to somewhat different conclusions. Some additional insight into
the nature of the population growth function may perhaps be attained
if we consider the problem of constructing a sub-model which attempts
to explain the shape of the population growth curve. This model is
based on particularistic assumptions that may or may not hold in the

real world. It is set out merely to illustrate an approach to the problem of model construction.

To begin with we introduce the notion of a role com-
plex.[11] A role complex is any set or collection of roles pertinent to
the phenomenon being studied. If the phenomenon under consideration
is fertility then we include only those roles in the role complexes
considered that in some way or other influence fertility. If the elimination of a role complex makes no difference to the determination
of the value of the variable being studied then it is excluded.

Now, individuals can be classified according to the
role complexes they inhabit. Or we may say that every individual is
characterized by a given role complex. Those inhabiting a given role
complex will adhere to values and rules of selection that determine
their behavior. We conceive of the population being distributed among
a finite number of unique role complexes. If for every role complex
there is associated with it a unique set of values and rules of selection then these, in conjunction with the parameters and biological
constraints that determine behavior, will determine the fertility of
the group characterized by that role complex.

We now turn to a slightly different aspect of the argument. It appears plausible that a shift in average income will cause,
or be associated with, a shift in the occupational structure. The exact nature of the shift in the occupational structure will depend, in
part, on the cause of the shift in income. Suppose that the cause is
an increase in the quantity of capital. The increase in capital will
cause a change in the proportion of the labor force attached to various
industries, since it is most likely that the increase in capital will
manifest itself more in some industries than in others. Associated
with the shift in the occupational structure there will most likely be
a shift in other aspects of the role structure. The exact nature of the
shifts that take place will depend, of course, on the particular circumstances.

We know, however, from some of the empirical information that has been gathered that, as average income rises, some

_____
[11] This is nothing more than a sector defined in a special way,
namely as a collection of roles.

of the shifts are likely to be of the following nature. (1) Initially there
will be a shift in population from rural to urban areas. (2) There is
likely to be a shift away from agriculture and into manufacturing enterprises. (3) Associated with increase in manufacturing enterprises
will be increases in commerce, communications, and transportation.[12]
Now, in urban occupations secular influences are likely to be stronger
and religious influences weaker, or so it is sometimes believed.
Furthermore, in urban centers marriages are likely to occur at later
ages and children are likely to be an economic burden rather than an
asset.

Now to get back to the central aspects of the argument.
The shift in role structures due to an increase in income is likely to
be from role complexes characterized by high fertility (of its members)
to role complexes characterized by potentially lower fertility. That
is, we assume that a given role complex is associated with a given
distribution of values and rules of selection, and that when people
shift from one role complex to another the groups that are characterized by those role complexes retain their proportionate distribution
of values and rules of selection even though the numbers in each group
have either grown or diminished.[13] If a lower proportion of those in
an expanding role complex group adhere to values that prohibit attempts
at birth control or sanction and put emphasis on rearing large families
than those in role complex groups which are contracting, then, other
things being equal, the birth rate will fall as the shift from one role
complex group to another takes place. At the same time increases in
average income are likely to have two other effects pertinent to present considerations. (1) Within any role complex group increases in
average income will result in reductions in the mortality rate -- the
age distribution being given. (2) Within some role complex groupings

---

[12] Cf. Colin Clark, op. cit.

[13] Strictly speaking, this is most unlikely to happen in the real world.
As people shift from one way of life (role complex) to another they
are most unlikely to change their values and rules of selection immediately. In time, however, the newcomers may take on some of the
outlook and ways of those that were previously in that role complex
grouping. The assumption made in the text above is an abstraction
that does not take into account the necessary period of adjustment.

increases in average income may, up to a point, promote increases in
fertility due to the better health and welfare often associated with
higher income levels, and through a reduction of the consequences of
the economic burden of having children. Since the fall in the mortality
rate for a given increase in average income is likely to be greater, at
first, than the probable reduction in the fertility rate, the end result
of this set of conditions is a population growth function in which the
rate of population growth is a monotonic increasing function of average income up to a point, beyond which, under the circumstances
specified below, the rate of population growth is a monotonic decreasing function of average income.

The reasons for this last conclusion may perhaps be
stated with greater clarity with the aid of a few symbols.

We begin with a given total population size at the start
of the period. Let Q_j denote the proportion of the total population in
the jth role complex grouping. There are n role complexes of which
j is the typical one. Also, let F_j denote the crude birth rate associated with role complex j. By F_j we mean the ratio of births attributable to role complex grouping j to the total population in that role
complex. It follows from these definitions that the ratio of total births
to the total population at the beginning of the period is

$$\sum_{j=1}^{n} Q_j \cdot F_j \qquad 14$$

---

14 That this formula really follows from the definitions may perhaps
be seen from the following. Let the total population size be designated
by P and total births by f. The ratio of births to total population is
f/P. Also, let the total births attributable to the jth role complex
grouping be designated by f_j and the population in the jth role complex grouping by P_j, so that

$$\sum_{j=1}^{n} f_j = f, \quad \text{and} \quad \sum_{j=1}^{n} P_j = P$$

Now, by definition,

$$F_j = \frac{f_j}{P_j}$$

and

$$Q_j = \frac{P_j}{P}.$$

Now, let M_j represent the crude mortality rate of those in role complex group j, by which we refer to the ratio of deaths of those in
group j to the total population in the group at the beginning of the
period. The crude mortality rate for the population as a whole is
therefore represented by

$$\sum_{j=1}^{n} Q_j \cdot M_j \quad {}^{15}$$

The rate of population growth can therefore be represented by

$$r = \sum_{j=1}^{n} Q_j \cdot F_j - \sum_{j=1}^{n} Q_j \cdot M_j$$

We now suppose that Q_j, F_j, and M_j, are all functions of average income. The nature of these functions is as follows.
As average income increases the net shifts in population are from
role complex groups associated with higher fertility rates to those
that have lower fertility rates so that there is a continuous increase

──────────

Hence,

$$F_j \cdot Q_j = \frac{f_j}{P}$$

Summing both sides of the last equation for all j we obtain

$$\sum_{j=1}^{n} F_j \cdot Q_j = \frac{\sum_{j=1}^{n} f_j}{P} = \frac{f}{P}$$

which is what we set out to show.

   It may perhaps be argued that the derivations in the text do not
take into consideration possible different age distributions within
each role complex grouping for different levels of average income.
This problem can probably be handled by subdividing each role complex grouping into age categories and applying to each age category
the appropriate fertility rate for that category. That is, C_i and F_i
are redefined so that they not only relate to those who inhabit a given
role complex but also to those who at the same time fall into a given
age category.

[15] By following the procedure indicated in the footnote above it can
readily be seen that this formula also follows from the definitions.

in the magnitudes of Q_j in the low fertility role complex groups and
a gradual decrease in magnitudes of Q_j in the high fertility role
complex groups. Also, for each group, up to a point, F_j increases
as average income increases, but the increases in F_j are at a decreasing rate. And last we suppose that M_j decreases as average
income increases, but that M_j decreases at a decreasing rate.

Now, what is the total effect of all those relationships
on the shape of the population growth function? The first effect of an
increase in income is to change the proportions belonging to various
role complexes. At first fertility may either increase, decrease, or
not change. There are two factors at work. The reallocation of
people to role complex groups for which fertility is lower works to
lower the crude birth rate. But for some groups increases in income
will, up to a point, stimulate increases in fertility, although the proportions belonging to these groups may be diminishing. But eventually
increases in income do not stimulate any more increases in F_j so
that, after some value of average income is reached, fertility must
drop because of the changes in the proportions belonging to various
role complexes. The decreases in mortality may be achieved in two
ways. First, within a given role complex group mortality is reduced
through increases in income; and second, there may be a redistribution of people to role complexes where mortality is lower. We thus
have two opposing effects generally: the one acting on mortality
causing increases in r, the other acting on fertility causing, after a
point, decreases in r. At first the forces acting to reduce fertility
may be insignificant due to the sluggishness of individuals to shift
from some groups to others when not many others are doing like-
wise, and second because at first average income rises may actually
induce increases in fertility within certain groups. The reductions in
mortality generally do not face similar hurdles. The outcome, with
respect to the rate of population growth, will of course depend on the
relative rates with which shifts from high fertility role complex
groups to low fertility role complex groups take place as against the
changing rates at which mortality decreases as average income increases. If the former rate does not decline, or does not decline as
rapidly as the latter rate, then eventually a level of average income
is reached at which the rate of population growth is a maximum, and

beyond which the rate of population growth declines.[16]

In the last analysis this example is, in a sense, completely arbitrary and can be no more than suggestive. It can only be hoped that the above remarks suggest something, if only vaguely, of the ways in which the basic models can be expanded.

---

[16] As average income increases the magnitude of r also increases as long as

$$\frac{d \sum\limits_{j=1}^{n} Q_j \cdot F_j}{dy} \qquad \frac{d \sum\limits_{j=1}^{n-} Q_j \cdot M_j}{dy}$$

where y is average income; and r is at a maximum if and when

$$\frac{d \sum\limits_{j=1}^{n} Q_j \cdot F_j}{dy} - \frac{d \sum\limits_{j=1}^{n} Q_j \cdot M_j}{dy}$$

CHAPTER IX

THE RELEVANCE, NATURE, AND SCOPE OF
OPTIMUM POPULATION THEORY

In any consideration of past theoretical work on the
interaction between demographic and economic forces one of the two
theories that immediately comes to mind is the optimum population
theory. It therefore appears reasonable to inquire how this theory
can contribute to the construction of a more adequate theory of demographic-economic development.

Our procedure will be as follows. First, an attempt
will be made to consider the various kinds of optimum population theories that can be conceived. This appears to be necessary since much
of the controversy about optimum population appears to have been at
cross purposes, with one author or group arguing in terms of one
possible version of the theory while a seemingly opposing author ar-
gues in terms of another possible version. It is unnecessary to enter
into any of the specific controversies, or points of controversy, in this
chapter since these are irrelevant to our major objectives. Second,
for purposes of orientation, an attempt will be made to restate briefly
some of the essential elements of optimum population theory. There
would appear to be little point in going beyond such a brief restate-
ment since there already exists a number of compilations of and detailed critiques on the existing literature.[1] (Furthermore, a new

---

[1] For a review of the literature see: E. F. Penrose, Population Theories and their Application, op. cit., pp. 47-91; Imre Ferenczi, The
Synthetic Optimum of Population. Geneva: League of Nations, 1938;
Manuel Gottlieb, "The Theory of Optimum Population for a Closed
Economy," Journal of Political Economy, Vol. 53, No. 4 (Dec., 1945),
pp. 289-316. These works contain, for most purposes, an adequate
number of bibliographical references.

and detailed analysis of the literature would be out of place since this
is not an essay on the history of doctrine.) Third, an attempt will be
made to reformulate optimum population theory on a somewhat higher
level of generality than has been done heretofore so that the nature of
the questions optimum theory deals with can be more clearly envisioned, and at the same time made somewhat more explicit. In this more
abstract formulation of the theory some additional conceptual tools
will be introduced.[2] Fourth, we shall attempt to find out what meaningful propositions (i.e. propositions that are conceivably falsifiable)
can be distilled out of the current optimum population theory. Last
we shall attempt to determine what place, if any, theories of optimum
population have in the development of a theory (or theories) of demographic-economic change. That is, we shall examine the kind of questions optimum population theory attempts to answer, what questions
it does not and cannot attempt to answer, and what relevance all of
this has to the construction of the kind of models described in the previous chapters.

The Variety of Optimum Population Theories

A number of different versions of optimum population
theory exist. An even larger number of versions are possible and conceivable. (If these two simple facts had been clearly recognized in the
past it seems likely that much fruitless controversy that has appeared
in the periodical literature could have been avoided.) Indeed, one of
the major difficulties in discussing optimum population theory is that
one is not always quite sure what it is.

Most of the existing versions probably fall into one of
two categories. They are either (1) single criterion static theories or
(2) multiple criteria static theories. The more frequently mentioned
criteria that come under the first category are: per capita real income,

---

[2] The concepts and reformulations developed below are not original
with the author. They have been used by others for other purposes in
other places. The application of some of these notions to a restate-
ment of optimum population theory is, as far as the author can tell,
quite new. In particular the author is indebted to Kenneth J. Arrow,
Social Choice and Individual Values, Cowles Commission Discussion
Paper No. 258; and Trygve Haavelmo, "The Notion of Involuntary
Economic Decisions," Econometrica, Vol. 18, No. 1 (Jan., 1950), pp.
1-8, for the notions of a weak ordering and collective choice, respectively.

per capita consumption, expectation of life, man-hour productivity, real wages per worker, etc. Some authors have argued that a single criterion should not be employed to the exclusion of all others. But any index composed of any combination of variables that are affected by population size can be proposed as suitable in choosing an index for the determination of the optimum population.

There are no dynamic theories of optimum population in the sense of theories that relate to processes of change over time. Although some recognition has been given to such factors as the exhaustion of resources, the discovery of new resources, or of new and more efficient uses for existing resources, the accumulation of capital, and the supposed volatility of the optimum point,[3] the mere recognition and consideration of these factors, without integration into a generalized framework, do not constitute, in the usual sense of the term, a dynamic theory. A truly dynamic theory would probably be concerned with the determination of an optimum population path, or optimum rates of change. Here again the index of welfare could depend on one variable or on some combination of many and hence a number of versions of dynamic optimum theory could conceivably be constructed.

The purpose of the above discussion is, for the most part, to indicate the variety of optimum theories that is possible, and the meaninglessness of speaking about the optimum population theory rather than of one of many versions.

A Brief Restatement of Optimum Population Theory

In the usual formulations of the economic optimum population theory only one criterion is used as an index of national well being or welfare. The usual index is per capita real income or something believed or assumed to be a monotonically increasing function of real income. We shall probably not misrepresent any of the important existing versions of optimum population theory if, in our brief expositions of the central elements of the theory, we employ per capita real income as our index of national welfare, and at the same time

---

[3] See Gottlieb, op. cit., pp. 302 ff. Also J. J. Spengler, "Aspects of the Economics of Population Growth," The Southern Economic Journal, Vol. 14, No. 2 (Oct., 1947), pp. 123-147 and Vol. 14, No. 3 (Jan., 1948), pp. 233-266.

assume that the ratio of labor force to total population remains constant.

The central notion of the theory is built upon the twin principles of the division of labor and the law of diminishing returns. Both of these principles when applied to an entire economy depend, in essence, on some notion of an aggregate production function. With a given resource base, given state of the arts, and given tastes, there exists a proportion of labor to other factors that will yield the greatest output per head. Any size less than that dictated by the ideal proportion will yield a lower output per capita because of the indivisibility of certain factors of production, and hence with a smaller labor force maximum use cannot be made of these indivisible factors, or less efficient factors and processes have to be employed. Beyond this ideal labor force size, each factor of labor has, on the average, less resources to work with, and hence per capita output would be lower than otherwise. We thus see that underlying the theory are the assumptions that (1) there exist indivisibilities of certain factors of production (at least one factor), and (2) that the quantity of other factors and the state of the arts are fixed at any one time. These are reasonable assumptions for a static theory. It also assumes, and this is less often noticed, that in some sense, people make the best use of the given resources and knowledge, or as an alternative, the theory must assume that with a greater population or lesser population no better use is made of existing resources and knowledge. Thus, the conquest of indivisibilities by a larger population, and the depressing effects of working with less capital per worker, lead to the conclusion that there is a population greater than which, or less than which, will yield a lower output per capita. Hence, if a population is permitted to grow beyond the optimum, and the optimum remains where it is, then the population will become, real-income-wise, worse off, and, of course, conversely if population size is smaller than the optimum and permitted to grow it will become better off. A knowledge of the functional relationship between population size and per capita income, or any other variable that is thought to be crucial would, if it could be obtained, presumably indicate whether a given population increase, under given conditions, is desirable or not.

In an economy that is not stationary, but is either expanding or contracting, the situation appears to be much more complex. For, at the same time that population size is changing other
crucial variables that affect per capita income are also changing.
Existing resources are being exhausted, new resources are being
discovered, new capital is being accumulated, and the state of the
arts is continually changing. Under conditions of this kind there is
little reason to believe that the optimum will remain stationary. If
the version of the theory considered admits volatility in the optimum
position then it follows that the ideal condition is for the population
size, at all times, to be identical with the optimum size, although this
would now be a moving point. Or, if this ideal movement of population size cannot be achieved then the gap between the moving actual
population size and the optimum population size should be such as to
minimize the difference between the welfare index at optimum size
and the same index at actual.

Before leaving this section it should perhaps be noted
that when changes over time enter the picture there are some nasty
problems of accounting for the effects of present activities on the
future income stream. However, these problems have not been solved
by the optimum theorists, and although they are highly significant we
cannot allow them to detain us here.

A Reformulation of the Optimum Population Size Problem

The theoretical aspects of the problem of determining
an optimum population size are much greater, it seems to the writer,
than the writings on optimum population would appear to indicate. It
need hardly be pointed out that the practical problems are enormous.
The ensuing reformulation of the theoretical aspects of the problem
is an attempt, in part, to reveal the nature and magnitude of the problem both from the points of view of statics and dynamics. The reader
should perhaps be warned that he will not find in the following few
pages a "solution" to the problem -- but rather, what will be indicated
is the nature of the questions that have to be answered for an optimum to be determined.

The Optimum Population Problem—Statics

It is convenient to distinguish between the problem of
determining an index of welfare -- or a welfare function -- and the

problem of determining the relationship between population size and other variables. The first question to be examined is therefore the question of the formulation of a welfare function.

With given resources, technology, and tastes, the size of population can be said to affect a set of variables X, whose elements are $X_1 \ldots X_n$. Now, the first notion to be considered is that of an "economic state" or "point." We define an "economic state" ("economic condition" might be an equally good term) as any set of values $x_1 \ldots x_n$ of the economic variables. For ease in communication let us call a given set of values that reflect an economic state a "point." (It can be viewed as a point in n dimensional space if there are n variables.) A point, then, is simply a description of a possible economic condition for a given unit period.

Now, in order to arrive at a welfare function it is necessary that the "society" be able to choose between points. That is, a necessary condition for the determination of a welfare function (and of an optimum population size) is that we be able to compare and order points, or economic states. Between two points a society must be able to choose whether it prefers the first, the second, or is indifferent between the two. This implies that it be possible to obtain at least a "weak ordering" for any set of points. By a weak ordering is meant a set of relationships between points such that between any two points w_1 and w_2, out of all possible points making up the set of possible economic states w, it can be said that either w_1 is preferred to w_2, w_2 is preferred to w_1, or that the society is indifferent between them. This is in contrast to a "strong ordering" in which the possibility of indifference is absent. In a strong ordering either w_1 is preferred to w_2 or w_2 is preferred to w_1.[4]

At this point a digression on the possibility of a

---

[4] A weak ordering also implies that the points in the set W have the properties of connectivity and transitivity. By connectivity is meant that if some relationship exists between w_1 and w_2, and if the same kind of relationship exists between w_2 and w_3, then this type of relationship exists between w_1 and w_3. If w_1 is preferred to w_2, and w_2 is preferred to w_3, then these three points are transitive if w_1 is preferred to w_3.

community ordering a set of economic states is appropriate. This is
a question that has plagued modern welfare economists. In the last
fifteen years or so economic welfare analysis has been reformulated
a number of times. On a number of occasions economists have suggested criteria that presumably did not contain any ethical bias whatso-
ever, but eventually it was pointed out that underlying each rule or
set of rules there really was one or more implicit ethical postulates
involved.[5] The upshot of this discussion appears to be that it $\underline{is}$
possible to formulate rules to order economic states, but that all of
these rules are arbitrary in the sense that they cannot be derived on
the basis of economic considerations alone. A brief review of some
of the principles that have been proposed will indicate something of
their nature.

(1) Given two economic states w_1 and w_2, if the
value of at least one element (variable) of w_1 is greater than the
corresponding element in w_2, and no element in w_1 is less than
the corresponding element in w_2, then w_1 is to be preferred to
w_2. However, a large number of comparisons may not be of this
nature and hence this rule may not be too helpful in many cases.

(2) Given two economic states w_1 and w_2, if at
least one member of the community feels that he is better off in w_1
than in w_2, and no one feels any worse off in w_1 than in w_2, then
w_1 is to be preferred to w_2.

(3) If, between two economic states w_1 and w_2,
those who prefer w_1 can pay those who prefer w_2 so that after the

---

[5] The literature on modern welfare economics is an expanding one.
An excellent review and critique of this body of literature can be
found in I. M. D. Little, "The Foundations of Welfare Economics,"
The Oxford Economic Papers, Vol. 1, No. 2 (June, 1949), pp. 227-247.
The five or six basic articles in this field are the following: Abram
Burk, "A Reformulation of Certain Aspects of Welfare Economics,"
Quarterly Journal of Economics, Vol. 52, No. 2 (Feb., 1938), pp. 310-
334; N. Kaldor, "Welfare Propositions in Economics," Economic
Journal, 1939, pp. 549-552; O. Lange, "The Foundations of Welfare
Economics," Econometrica, 1942, pp. 215-228; J. R. Hicks, "Founda-
tions of Welfare Economics," Economic Journal, 1939, pp. 696-712;
T. Scitovsky, "A Note on Welfare Propositions in Economics," Review
of Economic Studies, 1941, pp. 77-88. The literature is reviewed by
P. Samuelson, Foundations of Economic Analysis. Cambridge: Harvard
University Press, 1947, pp. 203-253. See also I. M. D. Little, A
Critique of Welfare Economics. Oxford University Press, 1951.

payment everyone prefers w_1, then w_1 is to be preferred to w_2.[6] (This is Kaldor's well-known compensation principle.) Kaldor has asserted that this principle holds even if no payments are made. While others (e.g. I. M. D. Little, cited above) have argued that the principle is meaningless if payments are not actually made.

(4) A seemingly more arbitrary procedure would be a direct or indirect (e.g. through elected representatives) voting rule of some sort.[7]

(5) Lastly, the ordering may be attempted by a governmental agency of some sort in one of two ways. (a) It may attempt an ordering that, as far as it can, will reflect, as far as possible, individual choice; or (b) no attempt may be made to reflect individual choice and the centralized choice may be imposed or dictated.

Although the above principles are arbitrary in one sense, they are not completely arbitrary in the sense that some rules are clearly inadmissible. For example, rules that contradict each other are inadmissible. Also, subsidiary rules not consistent with major principles are inadmissible. If certain ethical or moral precepts are granted as governing the rules, then rules that lead to results contradicting such precepts are inadmissible.

Finally, it may be said that if economic states cannot be ordered, then nothing can be said about optimum population theory, or about the application of any theory to economic policy. If we are to proceed at all with this matter, then it is necessary to proceed on the basis that the ordering of economic states, or points, is possible.

Now a given population size is consistent with one or more points (i.e. economic states). If every conceivable population size, denoted by $P_1 \ldots P_n$, is consistent with only one point then we can say that the population size uniquely determines the values of X.

---

[6] Scitovsky has suggested the additional condition that it must not be possible for those who prefer w_2 to pay those who prefer w_1 so that after the payment everyone prefers w_2. Otherwise we cannot really know whether w_2 is preferred to w_1 or vice versa.

[7] On the difficulties and implications of such a procedure see K. J. Arrow, Social Choice and Individual Values. New York: John Wiley, 1951.

But this is too rigid an assumption. We know from general experience that this is not likely to be the case. For example, a given population size may be consistent with more than one level of employment, more than one level of national income, more than one level of
investment, more than one level of per capita consumption, etc.;
these last may be X_j, X_k, X_1, X_m, in the set of variables X. If
this is true than it follows that any population size P_i is consistent
with a set of points, which is a proper subset of the set W whose
elements are all conceivable points w_i, for all i, to be considered.
Let us write W_j for the subset of W with which P_j is consistent.
We thus have for every population size P_1 ... P_n a corresponding
set of subsets, W_1 ... W_n. Any given point may be a member of more
than one subset. It is conceivable that some points may be members
of all the subsets W_j, for all j. However, a necessary condition
for an optimum to exist is that not all points must be members of all
subsets. That is, some points, at least one, must be unique to some
of the subsets and not to the others. Otherwise a given economic
state can be reached with any population size and hence there would
be no reason to prefer one population size to another. This condition
is of no practical significance since there is every likelihood that it
is always met with in practice.

From the subsets W_j, for all j, we form a new sub-
set W_j' whose elements (points) are preferred to all other elements
in W_j. It is clear that elements in W_j' cannot be preferred to each
other. Now, for each W_j' there is a corresponding population size
P_j for which the points in W_j' are possible points. It follows from
the transitivity condition that all points in any subset W_j' (j $\neq$.i),
that has an element (point) in common with W_i' cannot be preferred
to any point in W_i'.

We now define the set W' that consists of all the subsets W_j', for all j. Since a weak ordering exists among the elements
of W, and therefore among the elements of the subsets of W', we
can order the subsets of W' in terms of the ordering of their elements. That is, if every element of one subset is preferred to every
element of another, we can say that the first subset is preferred to
the second. Since the subsets of W' can be ordered, we can attach
ordinal values to each subset W_j' such that higher values go to

preferred subsets.

Now, in order to determine the optimum population
size we may posit a rule saying that the optimum population size (or
sizes) is that population size corresponding to the subset (or subsets)
in W' which has (have) the highest ordinal value. We should note,
however, that a rule of this kind places a particular interpretation on
the meaning of an optimum population, which, though not unreasonable,
is nevertheless arbitrary. Specifically, under this rule, the optimum
would be that population size which would permit the society the
opportunity of reaching the highest (most preferred) economic state
possible. The economic states represented by the points in W'_j are
only possible states and not necessarily the economic state that would
actually be achieved with the corresponding population size P_j. If we
view the operation of a particular economy as being of such a nature
that with a given population size the automatic functioning of the
economy will reach the most preferred economic state consistent with
that population size, then the rule under consideration loses its arbitrary characteristic. But there surely is little reason to believe that
economies function in this manner. In such a case it is conceivable
that the points in a subset of W', say W'_m, that are preferred to any
other subset in W', are such that it is highly improbable that any
one of them would be achieved, while some point in another subset
associated with another population size may actually be a better choice,
all things considered, because it is more likely to be achieved than
any point in W'_m, and is at the same time preferred to any other point
equally likely of achievement.

What we are saying, essentially, is that where a
community can with certainty achieve any point it may wish to achieve
then it is not arbitrary to order the subsets in terms of the most preferred point in each subset. On the other hand, where each economic
state cannot be achieved with certainty, but only with a certain probability, then it is arbitrary to do so. In those cases where we can
attach probabilities to the economic states, and hence to the elements
of each economic state in each subset, it may conceivably be possible
to compute an economic state for each subset that represents the expected value for each element of the economic states. Each subset,
W_j, will now be represented by a point (vector) whose components are

the expected values of the variables that define an economic state. The
subsets can now be ordered in terms of these representative points,
and the optimum population size will be that size (or sizes) corresponding to the subset (or subsets) containing the most preferred representative point.

The above procedure is reasonable only if it is possible
to assign probabilities to each point, and if the community is indifferent to risk. The community may prefer to have the opportunity to
reach a higher point rather than a lower one even if the odds are against
it. Or there may be no conceivable way of assigning probabilities to
points. In that case some other procedure for ordering the subsets
W_j would have to be discovered. That is, the community would face
the twofold problem of ordering the economic states, and ordering
the subsets W_j of these economic states.

Degrees of Freedom and Optimum Population

In our reformulation of the problem above we assumed
that a given population size is consistent with more than one economic
state. An assumption of this kind is related to our visualization of
the role of collective choice (or collective actions) in the system of
social and economic behavior, to the degrees of freedom in the system of equations that we visualize as determining the economic state,
and to the nature of the parameters we begin with. To clarify these
matters let us consider the notion of collective choice.

We conceive individual decisions as those decisions
made by individual units in society, where these units may be persons,
families, business firms, etc. By collective decisions we refer to
decisions made by the delegated representatives of the individual units
in the name of the collectivity of all the individual units. In Haavelmo's
analysis "collective action consists in invoking or maintaining a certain system or organizational form as far as the economic aspects of
the society are concerned."[8] Our notion is somewhat broader in that
we are not only concerned with invoking or maintaining a given organizational form but also with the ability of the collectivity, in the name
of the collectivity, to manipulate and affect certain variables in the
system, either directly or indirectly. Obviously, changes in organi-

---

[8] Haavelmo, op. cit., p. 5.

zational forms that do not affect the values of the variables are not of
much interest.

Consider a system of equations that reflect only individual decisions. Let us assume also, for the sake of exposition, that
the parameters are "real" or "natural" parameters; that is, that they
are determined by nature and cannot be changed by either individual
or collective action. Under these circumstances consider first a system of equations with zero degrees of freedom.

$$X_i = f_i (X_0, X_1, \ldots, X_{i-1}, X_{i+1}, \ldots, X_n), \quad i = 0, 1, \ldots, n.$$

where X_0 is population size, and $X_1, \ldots, X_n$ are the economic variables considered in our reformulation of the problem. Given that the
equations are independent and non-contradictory such a system consists of $n + 1$ equations in $n + 1$ unknowns. If we have in mind such
a system in discussing optimum population theory, then the theory,
even if applicable, cannot say anything of interest for policy purposes.
A knowledge of the optimum in a system where there are zero degrees
of freedom can only satisfy idle curiosity but can hardly be of any real
use. That is, the system above is a completely determined system
where only the equilibrium values are possible. If $\dot{x}_0$ happens to be
the value of X_0, and if $\dot{x}_0$ is in some sense or other "not optimum"
then it is unfortunate, but within such a completely determined system
nothing can be done. Under a completely determined system of this
kind it is nonsense to speak of optimum or non-optimum populations,
since only one population size is consistent with the values of the remaining variables. What is, is, and it has to be accepted, since the
system does not permit change to anything that is either better or
worse.

Consider now the slightly modified system of equations:

$$X_i = f_i (X_0, X_1, \ldots, X_{i-1}, X_{i+1}, \ldots, X_n), \quad i = 1, 2, \ldots, n.$$

We now have a system with one degree of freedom since
there are n independent and non-contradictory equations in $n + 1$
unknowns. If the population policy, and hence the value of X_0, is

determined by collective action, the system becomes determinate. Every value of X_0 implies one and only one economic state, although the various economic states implied by different values of X_0 need not all be different. Given an ordering of the economic states it is possible to determine the optimum population size. This case is simpler than the one discussed in the previous section, since one and only one economic state is consistent with a given population size.

Now imagine a system that contains two or more degrees of freedom. A given population size may now be consistent with more than one economic state. Collective action can now affect not only the size of the population but also the value of some other variables. In the real world this is unquestionably the case. For example, a government through its immigration laws, tax laws, laws with regard to public health and the dissemination of contraceptive information, may affect population size, the level of national income, income distribution, investment, etc.

The purpose of this discussion on degrees of freedom and collective action is to show that the concept of an optimum is closely related to what is achievable by collective action; and it is also related to our view of the system of equations we conceive as determining the economic state for a given period. Interpreting the equations as we did above, we must conclude that an optimum is meaningless in a system where there are zero degrees of freedom. Where there is only one degree of freedom, the optimum has a pretty concise meaning, if the economic states can be ordered. Where there is more than one degree of freedom, the problem is more complex since that involves not only ordering economic states, but possible sets of economic states. We conclude then that the optimum concept is meaningful only from the point of view of what is achievable by public action or public choice. That is, a population size may be said to be optimum if there does not exist a collective act such that, interacting with the individual choices, there will result a different population size and economic state which is preferred to the existing economic state.

Reformulation of the Optimum Population Problem - Dynamics

The determination of what may be called the dynamic

optimum of population is similar in many respects to the determination of the static optimum, except that we have to worry about "matrices"
rather than "points"; about "population paths" rather than population
sizes; and about achievable sequences of economic states and "dynamic consistencies" rather than merely achievable economic states.

In dynamics we are concerned with comparing possible
sequences of economic states rather than economic states for a given
unit period. Let us call a given sequence of economic states a
"matrix".[9] That is, we conceive of a matrix in which each column
vector represents what we previously called a point (or economic
state), and the column vectors are arranged in their natural time sequence. The rows, of course, represent the paths of the values which
the particular variables take on over time. The restrictions placed
on the elements of the matrix are that the sequence of values of any
variable must be consistent with (1) the initial conditions (and parameters) with which we start; and (2) the sequence of values taken on
by the other variables in the matrix.

The only matrices admissible for consideration are
those that are consistent with (1) the initial economic state, (2) the
resource base, (3) technological constraints and (4) institutional constraints. We begin with an economic state at time t_0. The other
columns in the matrix represent periods $t_1,...,t_i,...,t_n$. Now, any two
successive economic states, t_i and t_{i+1}, must be consistent with
each other in the sense that it must be possible for the state at t_{i+1}
to evolve out of t_i. Two kinds of consistency are required. The
magnitude of a given variable at t_{i+1} must be achievable in view of
the magnitudes of the other variables in the same economic state.
For example, investment at t_{i+1} plus consumption at t_{i+1} cannot
increase by more than the maximum increase in national income
possible. As long as no two consecutive economic states are incon-
sistent with respect to the above considerations, then the matrix may

---

[9] The term "matrix" is employed here rather loosely for want of a
better term. It is not used in its full mathematical sense in that not
all operations on these matrices (e.g. matrix multiplication) are
meaningful in this context.

be looked upon as an admissible matrix.[10]

Much of the analysis necessary for the determination of a dynamic optimum is similar to the analysis of static optimum theory and hence these aspects need not be considered again in detail, but can be treated with dispatch.

Having determined the set V of admissible matrices it is now necessary to visualize the possibility of a weak ordering of these matrices. The conditions and principles that are to hold here are similar to those considered above.

Just as in the static version we conceived of a given population size consistent with a subset of points, we now conceive of a given population <u>path</u> (or population-time function) $P_i(t)$ consistent with a subset of matrices v_i of the set V of all <u>admissible</u> matrices. By a population path we refer to a sequence of population sizes for the initial period t_0 and the periods that follow $t_1,....,t_i,....,t_n$. The initial population size is given. Only population paths that are conceivably achievable are admissible for consideration. That is, for any two consecutive time periods, t_i and t_{i+1}, the population size at t_{i+1} must be one that could conceivably grow out of the population size at t_i.. Any population size that can be accomplished by a collective choice is to be considered achievable.[11]

The rest of the analysis follows the same pattern as that employed in the reformulation of the problem of a static optimum. That is, out of each subset y_i we create a new subset y_i', for all i,

---

[10] A word should probably be said about the initial economic state at t_0. Since we have introduced the criterion that only conceivably achievable economic states are admissible, it follows that the initial state can only be that economic state actually in existence in the initial (present) period. In the present things are as they are and nothing can be done. Only the future can be different.

[11] This implies that the population size at t_{i+1} is also consistent with the age distribution, sex distribution, occupational distribution, etc., at t_i. Another point to be considered is that certain possible collective decisions may be considered inadmissible because they go against the moral values of the people involved; e.g. killing a portion of the population to achieve a certain size may not be an admissible collective choice.

whose members are preferred to all other matrices in y_i. The subsets y_i', for all i, compose the set V'. If the sequences of economic states represented by the matrices in V' can be achieved with
certainty then the optimum population path is that path consistent with
the subset in V' that is preferred to all other subsets in V'. If the
sequence of economic states represented by the most preferred
matrix (or matrices) cannot be achieved with certainty then the matter
of probability enters the picture, in which case the problem is the
same as it was for statics.

The analysis of the relationships between degrees of
freedom and optimum populations also follows along the same lines
for dynamics as it did for statics. Only the major conclusions of
such an analysis need be restated. (1) Where the system of equations
allows for no degrees of freedom then it is nonsense to speak of an
optimum population path since only one population path is possible.
(2) Where there is only one degree of freedom each subset v_i will
contain only one matrix and the optimum population path can be un-
ambiguously defined. (3) Where there is more than one degree of
freedom the subsets v_i and y_i' may contain more than one element
and the analysis can be carried on as above.

Some Conceivably Testable Propositions Derivable from Static Optimum Theory

We now return to the existing theory and inquire what
meaningful and conceivably testable propositions can be derived from
it? A meaningful proposition in an empirical science must contain
(a) definitions or terms that are operational in nature, and (b) assertions that are conceivably falsifiable. In the static version of optimum theory the meaningful propositions that can be derived are those
that say something about the nature of the population size-economic
welfare functions. These propositions are deducible from the twin
principles of the division of labor, and of diminishing returns.

One of the main assertions of the theory of an economic
optimum is that up to a point economic welfare is a monotonic non-
decreasing function of population size, and beyond that point it is a
monotonic non-increasing function of population size. If we make certain assumptions about the index of economic welfare, then we can say
something that is meaningful in the sense indicated above. For

example, assume that the index of economic welfare is per capita
real income under constant resources and techniques, where income
is defined in terms of a set of statistical operations. We can make
the following assertions:

(1) Given that $y_0P_1 > y_1P_1$ and $P_1 < P_2$ then $y_1P_2 \geq y_2P_2$;

or

(2) Given that $y_0P_1 > y_1P_1$ and $P_1 > P_2$ then $y_1P_2 \leq y_2P_2$;

or

(3) Given that $y_0P_1 < y_1P_1$ and $P_1 < P_2$ then $y_1P_2 \leq y_2P_2$;

or

(4) Given that $y_0P_1 < y_1P_1$ and $P_1 > P_2$ then $y_1P_2 \geq y_2P_2$;

where y and P are per capita real income and population size respectively, and where the subscripts indicate different time periods.[12]
The above would represent a set of testable propositions if (1) resources and production techniques remained constant for the period,
or if y_1 and y_2 are defined in such a way that the statistical operations defining y_1 and y_2 deflate per capita real income if resources
have decreased since period 0, and inflate per capita income if either
resources and/or techniques have improved since period 0. It follows

---

[12] The nature of the assertions may perhaps be seen more clearly
with the aid of the following diagrams that illustrate assertions (1)
and (4).

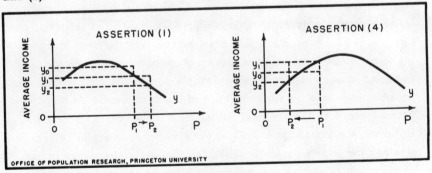

FIGURE 10

In the figures above the curve labelled y indicates
the levels of average income consistent with alternate population sizes. By comparing the relevant
areas in the figures above it can readily be seen
that the diagrams are in conformity with assertions
(1) and (4) in the text. Similar illustrations can be
constructed for assertions (2) and (3).

from the above that similarly meaningful theorems can be derived for
any other quantifiable index that is a monotonic transformation of per
capita income. Further, if the four propositions stated above proved
to be true empirically then we could conclude that in (1) and (4) the
population was moving away from the optimum, and in (2) and (3) the
population was moving toward the optimum.

The Scope and Relevance of the Existing Optimum Theory

When all is said and done, the scope of optimum population theory is, at best, exceedingly limited. This becomes clear when
we examine the kind of questions that optimum population theory does
not treat, especially with respect to the basic elements of a static or
dynamic theory outlined in the previous chapter. Going down the list
we find that optimum theory has nothing to say about the following:
(1) the nature of the roles and the role distributions pertinent to the
determination of population size; (2) the fields of action that can conceivably pertain to the process of demographic and economic changes;
(3) the role of values in the determination of population size; (4) the
choice-distributions or behavior equations that lead to different population sizes. In short, existing optimum population theory says
nothing about the determinants of population growth or decline, and
hence the theory can say little that is of interest for policy purposes
except when population happens to be the desired size. Otherwise the
static optimum is irrelevant. This follows from our conceptualization
of the notion of a dynamic optimum population path. The initial population size of a population path must be the existing one. If the existing population size is not the static optimum then an optimum has yet
to be achieved, which means following a population path of some sort,
which in turn implies the relevance of the dynamic optimum population
path approach to the problem rather than the static formulation.[13]
However, the static optimum concept may be relevant in determining
whether the initial population size is of an optimum nature or not.

For an economy in or close to Malthusian equilibrium

---

[13] An additional point that is often overlooked by writers on optimum
theory is that an optimum population size, if it is to be of any interest
for policy purposes, must be associated with a state of static equilibrium. Otherwise the desired state of affairs will be of a very fleet-
ing nature. Suppose that the economic state associated with a given
population size that is thought to be optimum is one that is consistent

the existing static optimum population theory has even less to say.
For in this case the major problem is how to escape from Malthusian,
or near Malthusian, conditions. The problem here is clearly dynamic
in nature. It involves two factors considered above: (1) the extent and
kind of collective action possible; and (2) the types and magnitudes of
displacers (and consequent displacements) available. For, as we have
argued, the optimum population path depends on what is achievable.
And the first thing that must be achieved is a sufficiently large positive displacement from equilibrium so that permanent rises in average income are possible. This simultaneously involves the question
of the degrees of freedom open to those groups or agencies that can
make effective collective choices. That is to say, it is important to
know to what extent collective action can affect the magnitudes of
savings, investment, capital-income ratios, fertility rates, mortality
rates etc., since, as we have seen, the magnitudes of these factors
determine, in part, whether or not the economy can escape permanently from Malthusian equilibrium. Once it is found that the escape from
Malthusian equilibrium is possible there then arises the complementary
question as to the kinds of collective action required in order to follow
an optimum population path.

Summary and Conclusions

In the main portions of this chapter we have attempted
to establish the following points:

(1) Although there are many versions of optimum theory
that are possible the existing versions are primarily static in nature.
The meaningfulness of the propositions that can be derived from existing optimum population theory depends on our ability to give an
operational description of the criteria used in the determination of an
optimum. It was shown that if the criterion employed was per capita
income, or some monotonic transformation of per capita income, then

---

only with a positive rate of population growth, while the optimum point
remains fixed, or moves in a direction opposite to that of the actual
population. Under such circumstances, if the optimum population size
is achieved it remains at the desired size for only a relatively short
period. This must be the case unless the theory implicitly assumes
that the rate of population change is independent of the economic state
of affairs.

a series of testable (i.e. conceivably falsifiable) propositions can be derived which would permit us to deduce whether a given population was approaching toward or departing from an optimum position.

In the case where a simple single criterion of welfare is not adopted then the problem is very much more complex. An attempt to indicate something of the nature and complexity of the problem of determining the conditions before a given population size can be declared as optimum was made above.

(2) In our reformulation of the problem we found it convenient to employ the notions of degrees of freedom, and collective action, and indicate the role of such ideas in a more accurate interpretation of the optimum concept. In doing so we have attempted to establish:

(a) That the notion of an optimum cannot accurately be employed apart from the specification of the system of equations that describes the determination of population size, and the economic state (or states) consistent with a given population size.

(b) That only where a collective act that can alter the population size is possible is it meaningful to speak of an optimum population. Where a social choice of this kind is not possible -- i.e. where the system envisaged has less than one degree of freedom -- the notion is meaningless.

(c) That the optimum depends on whether the desired results of collective action are certain (determinate) or only probable. If certain, then the optimum population size is that size (or those sizes) consistent with that set of achievable economic states preferred to all other achievable economic states, but if only probable then the determination is more complex. We may attempt to maximize the expected values of a set of possible outcomes, or not, depending on the possibility of assigning probabilities to the possible outcomes, and also depending on whether the community in question prefers to "play safe" rather than to take the opportunity to gamble for higher economic states.

(3) In the dynamic formulation of the problem the concepts of achievability and collective decisions become all the more prominent. These concepts enter the picture in two ways. First, they enter in the determination of what sequences of economic states and population sizes are admissible for consideration, since there is no

point in considering potential conditions that are impossible. Second,
these notions are closely tied to the application of theory to policy.
For example, in the case of an economy in or near Malthusian equilibrium a primary consideration is whether the possibilities for collective action are such as to achieve a sufficiently large displacement
from equilibrium for the economy to escape Malthusian conditions.
If that is possible then a simultaneous consideration is to determine
how the alternate possible collective choices affect population size
and other variables so as to determine the course of possible action
which would lead to an optimum population path.

CHAPTER X

SUMMARY AND FINAL REMARKS

Since the development, reconsideration, revision, and amendment of theories in the social sciences is an endless process a study of this sort can never be concluded. But at some point a temporary halt must be called and the results of research and speculation presented. At that point -- whatever the writer chooses to make it -- it is perhaps incumbent upon the author to say something on the possibly embarassing and perhaps impertinent queries that may be in the mind of the critical reader; namely: What of it? And where do we go from here?

In view of what has already been said it is certainly unnecessary at this point to defend attempts to construct concepts and fragments of theories in a field where so little theory exists. But what about the ideas developed in this particular essay, do they add up to anything? Out of the many facets of the process of economic development only those that involve significant demographic changes have been considered. Yet out of the seemingly disparate topics treated there emerges -- or so the writer believes -- the rough outline of a theory, which may be gleaned from a summary of the principle points.

1. A theory of demographic-economic development must begin somewhere. It has been suggested that a possible beginning can be made by examining the stability of the state of affairs that exists prior to development. If the state that we begin with is perfectly stable then long run development is out of the question. If development is possible then under some circumstances the equilibrium of the system is unstable. It therefore becomes necessary to examine those circumstances under which this is the case.

2. As a first step it was necessary to outline the nature

192

of an economy in demographic and economic equilibrium which reflected the conditions in that economy prior to what is generally understood as economic development. A model along Malthusian lines reformulated in modern terminology served this purpose. To this end
the principal conditions of Malthusian equilibrium were put forth in
Chapter II.

For development to take place there must be an initial
deviation from stationary equilibrium. Somehow things must get
started. As a first approximation, average real income was employed
as an index of economic development, and the course of development
was gauged by the extent to which average real income was above its
equilibrium level.

3. The next problem was to consider the factors which
could possibly stimulate an initial rise in average income. The initial
deviations from equilibrium average income were assumed to be caused
by events exogenous to the system. In particular three causative factors were considered. These were (a) injections of new capital into
the economy, (b) innovations, and (c) emigration. Events of this kind
were referred to as displacers, since they displaced average income
from its initial position.

4. Given an initial positive displacement from equilibrium average income what happens to the course of average income
over time? Does average income return to its equilibrium position
or does it continue to increase thereafter? To answer such questions
two simple dynamic models were suggested. In the first model it was
postulated that the rate of population growth was a monotonic increasing
function of average income up to a point, beyond which the rate remained at its maximum value. In the second model it was postulated that
above a certain level of average income the rate of population growth
declined. The models also designated certain income elevating factors and certain income depressing factors. If the initial displacement was positive then the major income elevating factors were the
proportion of the excess of average income over its equilibrium level
utilized for average net investment, and the extent to which an increase
in average capital resources increased average income. The income
depressing factors were the rate of population growth and the extent

to which a unit addition in population depressed average income if capital resources remained constant. On the basis of these models it was shown that the stability of Malthusian equilibrium depends (a) on the magnitude of the initial displacement (or on the magnitude of a series of displacements), and (b) on the relative magnitudes of the income increasing and the income depressing factors as average income varied from period to period.

On the basis of both models it was ascertained that Malthusian equilibrium possessed at all times stability in the small, and under some circumstances stability in the large with respect to average income. The major difference in conclusions in the results derived from the two models was that the system was unstable for sufficiently large displacements even under the adverse circumstances where the maximum product of the income raising factors (AB) was less than the maximum rate of population growth (r), if above a given level of average income the rate of population growth declined so that at some point it (r) was below the product of the income raising factors (AB).

5. It was argued that under certain plausible circumstances attempts to escape from Malthusian or near Malthusian conditions that failed would actually make the situation worse, in that future attempts to be successful would require greater displacements to achieve instability of equilibrium than would be necessary if the attempt that failed had never taken place.

Also, it was demonstrated that under some circumstances a series of displacements strategically spaced through time would be more effective than a given single large displacement of equal magnitude.

6. In order to escape from Malthusian conditions a country may attempt to act in one or more of three directions: (a) it may attempt to obtain as large a displacement (or series of displacements) as possible; (b) it may attempt to increase the magnitude of the income raising factors; and (c) it may attempt to decrease the magnitude of the income depressing factors. With respect to the last two points it becomes necessary to understand the determinants of the income elevating and the income depressing factors. Some suggestions were made about the construction of auxiliary models that would

conceivably explain the determination of the income raising and income depressing factors. It was argued that the effects of activities
between various sectors of the economy are exceedingly important in
determining the extent of the income raising and income depressing
factors. To this end the problems involved in the construction of
multi-sector models were examined, and the effects of different patterns
of population and investment shifts analyzed.

Ultimately, a complete explanation of the process of
demographic-economic change must get down to the "micro" level.
That is to say, at some point the explanation must be in terms of the
individual decision making process and of the technological and biological constraints that are involved. Various aspects of the problem
of developing explanations at this level were analyzed.

7. With respect to the determination of the population
growth function it was argued that human values (or mores) are an
important determining factor. It was pointed out that such values can
be conceived as the rules of selection, or part of the description of
the rules of selection, between alternatives. Also, a procedure was
outlined by which the distribution of values in a society could be described numerically, and through which values could be expressed and
integrated into more general schemes.

8. In the final substantive chapter certain questions related to optimum population theory were investigated. The major conclusions reached here were: (1) that the existing static optimum population theory had little to offer toward the construction of a theory of
demographic-economic development; (2) that apart from the situation
in which the existing population was already of an optimum size the
important problem was the determination of an optimum population
path rather than the achievement of a population of a certain size; (3)
that such an optimum path depends on what is achievable, which in turn
depends on the degrees of freedom in the system of equations which we
view as a description of the determination of the magnitudes of the
variables. Furthermore, with respect to the problems faced by areas
in or near Malthusian equilibrium the existing optimum theory has
particularly little to say since, in this case, the first problem is the
achievement of a displacement (or series of displacements) sufficiently large that the area can escape permanently from Malthusian

conditions. Whether this last can or cannot be done depends on considerations discussed above, and on the collective choices open to the
economy.

With this summary only a little more need be said on
the question, what of it? Implicitly the problems we are concerned
with are the problems of poverty, starvation, and early death, and the
possibilities of eliminating these conditions. The extent to which an
essay of this sort is of interest is determined in part by the light it
can shed on such problems. But the light that an incomplete theory
can shed depends on the extent to which it contains or leads to important propositions that have empirical validity. And to determine
whether such propositions can be derived from the theory requires
further efforts of both a theoretical and empirical nature. Which, in
part, explains our interest in the query, where do we go from here?
But what can one say in this connection that is neither obvious nor
banal?

The usual procedure in essays or treatises of a theoretical character is to leave the verification of the theory to others --
that is, to the statisticians, demographers, econometricians, and
economic historians. This is a customary division of labor. Sometimes others take up the challenge, often they do not. At one time the
writer hoped that in this essay he would deviate from this custom. He
planned to outline in the final chapter a program for the extension of
the theory and the verification (by which, in the positivist tradition,
we mean unsuccessful attempts at disproof) of the major propositions.
Upon further reflection it appears that such an outline probably could
not be stated within the usual length of a chapter, and in any event it
would probably be a vain and presumptuous undertaking. The determination of future research is too complicated a question to be considered here, and furthermore it involves considerations beyond the
scope of this essay. However, a few brief remarks indicating some
of the areas that the author would look into, if he did not choose
temporarily to stop his investigation at this point, may be of interest.

In connection with the problems we are considering
there are at least three areas we believe to merit additional attention.
These are: (1) Empirical research which leads to an evaluation of the
postulates considered, and further leads to the determination and

development of a set of workable postulates that are closer approxi-
mations to reality than the ones employed; (2) empirical investigations
which yield additional knowledge about the relative importance of variables worthy of consideration in an explanation of the process of economic growth; and (3) an evaluation of the existing models and the
possible construction of new models based upon findings uncovered
under (1) and (2). The reader interested in the empirical validity of
the propositions developed in this essay may be surprised by the con-
spicuous absence from the above list of any immediate interest on the
part of the writer to test such propositions. These comments call for
some elaboration.

We saw that in many aspects of the problem there are
alternate reasonable postulates upon which a theory can be built. It
follows that investigations which lead to a narrowing of the range of
alternatives are desirable. Such a narrowing of the possibilities can
be accomplished if we could obtain the answers to a number of questions
about values, attitudes, and mores, that come to mind. For example,
what do we postulate with respect to the distribution of values and attitudes that help to determine family size? What do we assume about
the tenacity with which such values are held? To what extent and in
what way do changes in the economic environment affect people's
attitudes in this respect? How do traditional attitudes about the worth-
whileness of different occupations affect resistance to occupational
mobility? What attitudes do people have toward investment and in what
way do such attitudes affect the pattern of investment shifts? On some
of these questions there exists a large body of information of an im-
pressionistic character, as well as some statistical information, that
we may hope can throw some light on the problem of choosing the best
hypotheses. Although the tasks of examining and carefully evaluating
the existing literature with this end in view, and of doing the supple-
mentary empirical investigations that may appear appropriate in order
to fill the gaps in the existing information would be far from simple
they are likely to be rewarding from the standpoint of assessing the
utility and realism of alternative postulates.

We saw in other portions of this essay that the more
aggregative the model the less the number of variables that need be
employed, and the less aggregative the model the more the number of

variables that need be considered. This is not a hard and fast rule but generally it appears to be the case. Now, no model includes all the variables involved in the real situation. Therefore, the more "micro" the model, if we may use such a phrase, the larger the number of variables likely to be left out in model construction, and the more important it is to be able to assess the significance of different variables. We would expect that additional empirical and statistical research would lead to a better selection of variables and relationships than those found in this essay. In any event it is a matter worth checking. We would further expect that discoveries resulting from such investigations would lead to the extension and probable revision of the existing theory.

Finally, a word need be said about the author's belief that it is premature to attempt to outline at present the manner in which the propositions developed in this essay can conceivably be tested. This belief is based on the view that scientific propositions of the kind we have in mind can be tested only if they lead to predictions which turn out to be either true or false. But the problem of prediction in a quantitative science involves the problem of measurement. At present it is probable that many of the measurements and computations necessary for prediction cannot be made, either because the necessary statistics have not been collected, or are at present not collectable, or because the required techniques of measurement have not been developed. If the measurements and consequent predictions cannot be made then there is little chance of testing the assertions we have tried to establish. If at some future time the measurements and statistics necessary for prediction are developed, it is likely that by that time a more adequate theory would be evolved, so that the propositions investigators will find it worth while to test will be those derived from a more embracing theory of economic development. As a consequence it appears that to attempt to suggest means of testing propositions developed in this essay is, at present, otiose.

BIBLIOGRAPHY

ARROW, KENNETH J., Social Choice and Individual Values, Cowles Commission Discussion Paper No. 258. Chicago: The Cowles Commission, 1950. (Hectographed)

BEAN, LOUIS H., "International Industrialization and Per Capita Income," Part V, pp. 119-144 in: Conference on Research in Income and Wealth, Studies in Income and Wealth, Vol. 8. New York: National Bureau of Economic Research, 1946.

BLACK, JOHN D., "Agricultural Production in Relation to Agricultural Resources," Annals of the American Academy of Political and Social Science, Vol. 188 (Nov., 1936), pp. 205-217.

BLOOM, G. F., "Note on Hicks's Theory of Invention," American Economic Review, Vol. 36, No. 1 (March, 1946), pp. 83-96.

BONAR, JAMES, Malthus and His Work. New York: The Macmillan Co., 1924.

BONAR, JAMES, Theories of Population from Raleigh to Arthur Young. London: G. Allen and Unwin, 1931.

BOULDING, KENNETH E., "Professor Tarshis and the State of Economics," American Economic Review, Vol. 38, No. 1 (March, 1948), pp. 93 ff.

BOWEN, H., "Capital in Relation to Optimum Population," Social Forces, Vol. 15, No. 3 (March, 1937), pp. 346-350.

BURK, ABRAM, "A Reformulation of Certain Aspects of Welfare Economics," Quarterly Journal of Economics, Vol. 52, No. 2 (Feb., 1938), pp. 310-334.

CARR-SAUNDERS, A. M., World Population. London: Oxford University Press, 1936.

CASSELS, JOHN M., "On the Law of Variable Proportions," in: Readings in the Theory of Income Distribution. Philadelphia: The Blakiston Co., 1946.

CHEN, TA, Population in Modern China. Chicago: University of Chicago Press, 1946.

CLARK, COLIN, Conditions of Economic Progress. London: The Macmillan Co., 1940.

CLARK, COLIN, The Economics of 1960. New York: The Macmillan
Co., 1942.

CLARK, J. M., Preface to Social Economics. New York: Farrar and
Rinehart, Inc., 1936.

CONNELL, K. H., "Land and Population in Ireland, 1780-1845," The
Economic History Review, Second Series, Vol. 2, No. 3 (1950),
pp. 278-289.

DAVIS, KINGSLEY, Human Society. New York: The Macmillan Co.,
1949.

DOMAR, E. D., "The Problem of Capital Accumulation," American
Economic Review, Vol. 38, No. 5 (Dec., 1948), pp. 777-794.

DOUGLAS, PAUL H., The Theory of Wages. New York: The Macmillan
Co., 1934.

DUBLIN, LOUIS I., Population Problems in the United States and
Canada. New York: Houghton, Mifflin Co., 1926.

DUESENBERRY, JAMES S., Income, Saving, and the Theory of Consumer Behavior. Cambridge, Mass.: Harvard University Press,
1949.

FAIRCHILD, HENRY P., "Optimum Population," in: Mrs. Margaret
Sanger (ed.), Proceedings of the World Population Conference.
London: E. Arnold and Co., 1927.

FERENCZI, IMRE, The Synthetic Optimum of Population. Geneva:
League of Nations, 1938.

FIELD, JAMES ALFRED, Essays on Population. Chicago: University
of Chicago Press, 1931.

FISHER, A. G. B., "Production, Primary, Secondary, and Tertiary,"
Economic Record (June, 1939), pp. 24-38.

FRISCH, R., "On the Notion of Equilibrium and Disequilibrium," Review
of Economic Studies, Vol. 3, No. 2 (Feb., 1936), pp. 100-105.

FROMONT, PIERRE, Demographie économique. Paris: Payot, 1947.

GHOSH, D., Pressure of Population and Economic Efficiency in India.
London: Oxford University Press, 1946.

GLASS, D. V., Population Policies and Movements. London: Oxford
University Press, 1940.

GLENDAY, ROY, "Long-Period Economic Trends," Journal of the
Royal Statistical Society, Vol. 101, No. 3 (1938), pp. 511-552.

GONNARD, RENE, Historie des doctrines de la population. Paris: Nouvelle Librairie Nationale, 1923.

GOTTLIEB, MANUEL, "The Theory of Optimum Population for a Closed Economy," Journal of Political Economy, Vol. 53, No. 4 (Dec., 1945), pp. 289-316.

HAAVELMO, TRYGVE, "The Notion of Involuntary Economic Decisions," Econometrica, Vol. 18, No. 1 (Jan., 1950), pp. 1-8.

HANSEN, ALVIN H., "Extensive Expansion and Population Growth," Journal of Political Economy, Vol. 48, No. 4 (Aug., 1940), pp. 583-585.

HARROD, R. F., Towards a Dynamic Economics. London: The Macmillan Co., 1948.

HECKSCHER, E. F., "Swedish Population Trends Before the Industrial Revolution," The Economic History Review, Second Series, Vol. 2, No. 3 (1950), pp. 266-277.

HICKS, J. R., "Foundations of Welfare Economics," Economic Journal, Vol. 49, No. 196 (Dec., 1939), pp. 696-712.

HICKS, J. R., Value and Capital. Oxford: Clarendon Press, 1946.

HOOD, W. C., "Some Aspects of the Treatment of Time in Economic Theory," The Canadian Journal of Economics and Political Science, Vol. 14, No. 4 (Nov., 1948), pp. 453-468.

INTERNATIONAL LABOUR OFFICE. Preparatory Asiatic Regional Conference, The Economic Background of Social Policy Including Problems of Industrialization. New Delhi: I. L. O., 1947.

ISAAC, JULIUS, Economics of Migration. New York: Oxford University Press, 1947.

JAFFE, A. J., "Technological Innovations and the Changing Socio-Economic Structure," Scientific Monthly, Vol. 67, No. 2 (Aug., 1948), pp. 93-102.

KALDOR, N., "Welfare Propositions in Economics," Economic Journal, Vol. 49, No. 195 (Sept., 1939), pp. 549-552.

KEYNES, J. M., The General Theory of Employment, Interest, and Money. New York: Harcourt, Brace and Co., 1936.

KNIGHT, FRANK, The Ethics of Competition. New York: Harper and Bros., 1935. (Chapter 6.)

KOOPMANS, T., "Identification Problems in Economic Model Construction," Econometrica, Vol. 17, No. 2 (April, 1949), pp. 125-144.

LANDRY, A., Traite de demographie. Paris: Payot, 1945.

LANGE, O., "The Foundations of Welfare Economics," Econometrica, Vol. 10, No. 3-4 (July-Oct., 1942), pp. 215-228.

LINDAHL, ERIK, Studies in the Theory of Money and Capital. London: Allen [1939]. (Part I: "The Dynamic Approach to Economic Theory.")

LINDBERG, JOHN, "Food Supply Under a Program of Freedom From Want," Social Research, Vol. 12, No. 2 (May, 1945), pp. 181-204.

LINTON, RALPH, The Study of Man. New York: D. Appleton-Century Co., 1936. (Chapter VIII, "Status and Role.")

LITTLE, I. M. D., "The Foundations of Welfare Economics," The Oxford Economic Papers, Vol. 1, No. 2 (June, 1949), pp. 227-247.

MALTHUS, T. R., An Essay on the Principle of Population (rev. ed.). London: The Everyman Library [no date].

MALTHUS, T. R., "Population," Encyclopaedia Britannica, Supplement to the Fifth Edition.

MANDELBAUM, K., The Industrialization of Backward Areas. London: Oxford University Press, 1945.

MARSCHAK, J., "Identity and Stability in Economics: A Survey," Econometrica, Vol. 10, No. 1 (Jan., 1942), pp. 61-74.

MOORE, WILBERT E., Economic Demography of Eastern and Southern Europe. Geneva: League of Nations, 1945.

MYRDAL, G., "Industrialization and Population," in: Economic Essays in Honour of Gustav Cassel. London: Allen and Unwin, 1933.

NOTESTEIN, FRANK W., "Population -- The Long View," in: Theo. W. Schulz (ed.), Food for the World. Chicago: University of Chicago Press, 1945.

NOTESTEIN, FRANK W., and others, Demographic Studies of Selected Areas of Rapid Growth. New York: Milbank Memorial Fund, 1944.

OLSON, E. C., "Factors Affecting International Differences in Production," American Economic Review, Vol. 38, No. 2 (May, 1948), pp. 502-522.

PARSONS, TALCOTT, The Structure of Social Action. New York: McGraw-Hill, 1937.

PATTON, F. LESTER, Diminishing Returns in Agriculture. New York: Columbia University Press, 1926.

PENROSE, E. F., Population Theories and their Application. Stanford University, Calif.: Food Research Institute, 1934.

PETERSON, GEORGE M., Diminishing Returns and Planned Economy.
    New York: Ronald Press, 1937.

PIGOU, A. C., The Economics of Welfare. London: The Macmillan
    Co., 1938.

PITT-RIVERS, G. H. L. F. (ed.), Problems of Population. London:
    G. Allen and Unwin, 1932.

PLUMMER, ALFRED, "The Theory of Population: Some Questions of
    Quantity and Quality," Journal of Political Economy, Vol. 40, No.
    5 (Oct., 1932), pp. 617-637.

ROBBINS, L., "The Optimum Theory of Population," in: T. E. Gregory
    and H. Dalton (eds.), London Essays in Economics. London:
    Routledge, 1927.

ROBINSON, JOAN, "The Classification of Inventions," Review of
    Economic Studies, Vol. 5, No. 2 (Feb., 1938), pp. 139-142.

ROSENSTEIN-RODAN, P. N., "Problems of Industrialization of
    Eastern and South-Eastern Europe," Economic Journal, Vol. 53,
    No. 210-211 (June-Sept., 1943), pp. 202-211.

SAMUELSON, P. A., Foundations of Economic Analysis. Cambridge,
    Mass.: Harvard University Press, 1947.

SAUVY, ALFRED, Richesse et population. Paris: Payot, 1943.

SCHELLING, T. C., "Capital Growth and Equilibrium," American
    Economic Review, Vol. 37, No. 5 (Dec., 1947), pp. 864-876.

SCITOVSKY, T., "A Note on Welfare Propositions in Economics,"
    Review of Economic Studies, Vol. 9, No. 1 (Nov., 1941), pp. 77-88.

SPENGLER, J. J., "Aspects of the Economics of Population Growth,"
    Southern Economic Journal, Vol. 14, No. 2 (Oct., 1947), pp. 123-
    147 and Vol. 14, No. 3 (Jan., 1948), pp. 233-266.

SPENGLER, J. J., "Pareto on Population, I," Quarterly Journal of
    Economics, Vol. 58, No. 4 (Aug., 1944), pp. 571-601.

SPENGLER, J. J., "Population and Per Capita Income," Annals of the
    American Academy of Political and Social Science, Vol. 237
    (Jan., 1945), pp. 182-192.

SPENGLER, J. J., "Some Effects of Changes in the Age Composition
    of the Labor Force," Southern Economic Journal, Vol. 8, No. 2
    (Oct., 1942), pp. 157-175.

SPENGLER, J. J., "The World Hunger -- Malthus, 1948," Proceedings
    of the Academy of Political Science, Vol. 23, No. 2 (Jan., 1949),
    pp. 53-71.

STIGLER, GEORGE, "Production and Distribution in the Short Run," Journal of Political Economy, Vol. 47, No. 3 (June, 1939), pp. 305-327.

THOMAS, DOROTHY SWAINE, Social Aspects of the Business Cycle. London: Routledge, 1925.

THOMPSON, WARREN S., Population and Peace in the Pacific. Chicago: University of Chicago Press, 1946.

TINBERGEN, JAN, The Dynamics of Business Cycles. Chicago: University of Chicago Press, 1950. (Chapter 9.)

UNITED KINGDOM, Royal Commission on Population, Report. London: H. M. Stationery Office, 1949.

UNITED NATIONS, Findings of Studies on the Relationships Between Population Trends and Economic and Social Factors. (Population Division, Report to the Secretariat.) Lake Success, 1950.

UNITED NATIONS, World Population Trends, 1920-1947. Lake Success, 1949.

VANCE, RUPERT B., "Malthus and the Principle of Population," Foreign Affairs, Vol. 26, No. 4 (July, 1948), pp. 682-692.

VIANELLI, SILVIO, "A General Dynamic Demographic Scheme and Its Application to Italy and the United States," Econometrica, Vol. 4, No. 3 (July, 1936), pp. 269-283.

WARRINER, DOREEN, Economics of Peasant Farming. London: Oxford University Press, 1939.

WOLFE, A. B., "The Population Problem Since the World War, A Survey of Literature and Research," Journal of Political Economy, Vol. 36, No. 5 (Oct., 1928), pp. 529-559 and Vol. 36, No. 6 (Dec., 1928), pp. 662-685.

WRIGHT, HAROLD, Population. (Cambridge Economic Handbooks.) New York: Harcourt, Brace and Co., 1923.